CULTURES OF THE WORLD

PORTUGAL

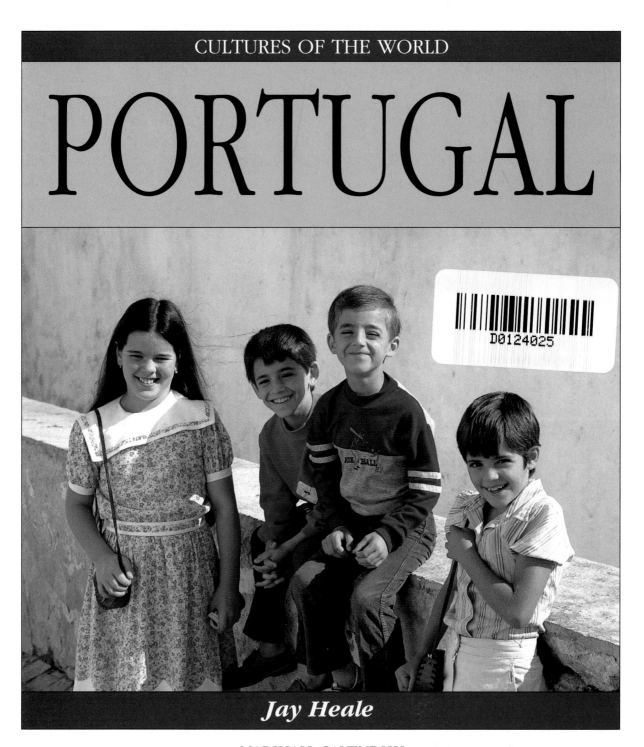

Jay Heale

MARSHALL CAVENDISH
New York • London • Sydney

Reference edition published 1995 by
Marshall Cavendish Corporation
2415 Jerusalem Avenue
P.O. Box 587
North Bellmore
New York 11710

© Times Editions Pte Ltd 1995

Originated and designed by
Times Books International, an imprint of
Times Editions Pte Ltd

Printed in Singapore

Library of Congress Cataloging-in-Publication Data:
Heale, Jay.
    Portugal / Jay Heale
      p. cm.—(Cultures Of The World)
    Includes bibliographical references (p.) and index.
    ISBN 0-7614-0169-5 (Portugal)
    ISBN 0-7614-0167-9 (Set)
    1. Portugal—Juvenile literature. [1. Portugal] I. Title.
II. Series.
DP517.H4 1995
946.9—dc20   94–43351
               CIP
                 AC

Cultures of the World

Editorial Director	Shirley Hew
Managing Editor	Shova Loh
Editors	Elizabeth Berg
	Dinah Lee
	Azra Moiz
	Sue Sismondo
Picture Editor	Susan Jane Manuel
Production	Anthoney Chua
Design	Tuck Loong
	Felicia Wong
	Loo Chuan Ming
	Wendy Koh
Illustrators	Chow Kok Keong
	Anuar bin Abdul Rahim
MCC Editorial Director	Evelyn M. Fazio

INTRODUCTION

A GENTLE COUNTRY, temperate in weather and mood, Portugal is surprising in its variety. Vivid contrasts of scenery, striking art styles, beautiful buildings, and proud relics of history are crammed into this narrow corner of the Iberian peninsula.

There was a time in its history when Portugal was reaching out to the world—a time of Prince Henry the Navigator and the explorer Vasco da Gama, a time when the pope divided the undiscovered world between Portugal and Spain. Then there was a time of equally spectacular decline when Portugal was content to be cut off from the world, a time of struggling self-sufficiency, of monarchs and dictatorship, of poverty. Now Portugal is hesitantly reaching out once more—not to build an empire, but to join the European world. There is still a stark division between rich and poor, but there is also a fresh determination to modernize and improve a struggling economy.

CONTENTS

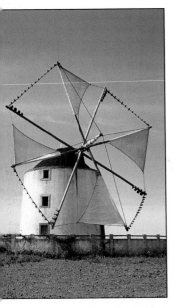

Typical Portuguese wind-mill used by farmers to grind grain and bring water to the land.

CONTENTS

Woman in widow's black.

GEOGRAPHY

PORTUGAL ONCE HELD dominion over colonies in South America, Africa, India, and China. As recently as 1957, 1,360,000 square miles (3,522,000 sq km) of world territory were ruled by the Portuguese. Today, a glance at the map of Europe reveals Portugal only as a rectangular strip at the southwestern corner of the Iberian peninsula, four-fifths of which is Spain. But no map can fully reveal the spectacular geographical and climatic variations within those borders: coastline, high mountains, fertile valleys, and spreading plains.

Continental Portugal covers 34,317 square miles (88,880 sq km); 362 miles (580 km) from north to south, and no more than 150 miles (240 km) from east to west at its widest point (about the same size as the state of Indiana). Its population is just over 10 million, including the islands of the Azores and Madeira, which are all that remain of Portugal's once extensive empire.

Opposite: **Lilies growing wild in the Algarve.**

Left: **Rugged mountains and fertile plains in a country where large families depend on their farms for a living.**

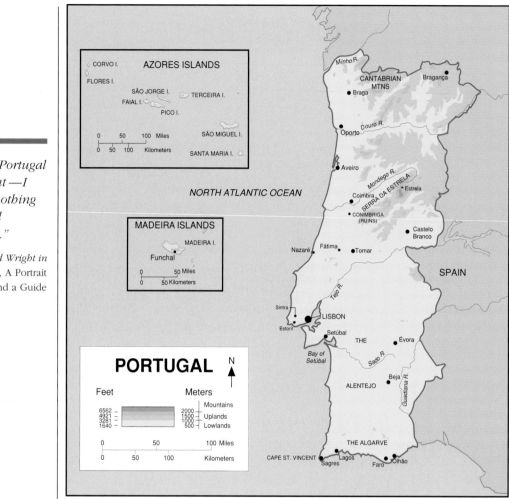

CLIMATE

Hot, dry summers and short, mild winters are normal for most of the central areas. The western coastline enjoys cool evening breezes. Westerly winds and the surrounding waters provide much of Portugal with cool, damp weather in the winter months of December and January, although inland the northern mountains of Serra da Estrêla can get snow. The average annual rainfall is 46 inches (116.8 cm) in the northwest vine-growing country and 27 inches (68.5 cm) in the capital city of Lisbon. The inland plains are virtually rainless through the summer months.

COSTA VERDE

The "Green Coast" of the northwest is so called because of its vineyards and pine forests. Oporto, the second largest city in Portugal, gives its name to the most famous wine of the country—port. Tripe is the speciality of the local menu, so the citizens of Oporto are known jokingly as *tripeiros* ("tri-PEY-ross," or little tripe). The locals tell how all the cattle in the region were killed to feed the fleet of Prince Henry the Navigator, leaving the citizens with only the entrails (tripe). True or not, they cook it frequently, with beans in steaming casseroles.

Inland, vineyards crowd the rugged valley of the River Douro (meaning River of Gold). It is difficult earth in which to grow vines, but nowhere else in the world can real port be produced. So terraces 25 to 30 feet wide have been carved out of the steep green hillsides that rise above the winding river. Every row of vines is important. Grapes grow everywhere, hanging from trees, porches, and even across narrow streets, while pockets of corn and olive trees fight for fertile space.

Vineyards in the Douro valley, famous for its grapes and wines.

OPORTO

Its name (though the Portuguese usually drop the 'O' and call it Porto) means simply The Port: the area nearby was called *Portucale*, which became the name of the kingdom and then of the country. From its courage in fighting off the Moors and later the armies of Napoleon, Oporto assumes the title of "The Unconquered City."

It is a busy commercial city, with prosperity and poverty existing side by side. Home of the port wine trade, it is built on steep hills on the north bank of the Douro River. Somewhat shabby granite buildings stare down on the busy, fishy-smelling waterfront. The river is spanned by two spectacular bridges. The single-span rail bridge was designed by Gustave Eiffel, whose metal tower dominates Paris. The two-tiered Dom Luis road bridge joins the commercial city center with the south bank of the Douro, where opulent port wine lodges show off the prime product of the area.

Further inland is the Minho, a mountainous spread of blue hills, green meadows, fruit orchards and olive groves, and carefully kept vineyards. The village folk live in sturdy, limewashed cottages built of granite slabs. There is usually a large room below with space for the storage of wine. The main town is Braga, whose narrow main street leads past old-fashioned shopfronts with tiny ironwork balconies, to its huge Romanesque cathedral. The palace of the Archbishop of Braga houses one of the largest libraries in the country.

The mountain town of Guimarães is the birthplace of Portugal. From here, Afonso Henriques, the country's first king, launched his defeat of the Moors, who had all but overrun the land. Here, where "the soul of Portugal was born," the old streets are so narrow that they remain cool and shadowy on the hottest day. To the north, near the Spanish border, the woods of Serra Geres, rich with oak, quince, cedar, chestnut, pine, and maple, are popular for walking.

COSTA DE PRATA

The main Atlantic coastline between Lisbon and Oporto is known as the "silver coast." The area is rich with history, made richer by tourism. The traditional fishing village of Nazaré has grown into an over-decorated tourist trap, where the fishing boats are garishly painted and the locals wear traditional clothing to earn a tip. Once, fishers rolled their boats across the beach on wooden rollers, rowed out to sea, dropped their nets, and then used teams of oxen to haul the nets in. Today, tractors and cranes make the fishing trade more efficient and less romantic.

The town of Aveiro is situated on a saltwater lagoon of the River Vouga delta, crisscrossed by canals spanned by humpbacked bridges. It is called the Portuguese Venice. Also in this region is the walled town of Obidos, a bridal gift from the king of Portugal, Dom Dinis, to his queen. The region also contains the pilgrimage town of Fátima, and Tomar with its fortified castle built by the great Crusading Order of the Knights Templar.

Coimbra, an ancient town of narrow, cobbled streets, was founded by the Romans and occupied by the invading Moors until the 11th century. It was the capital of Portugal in the 12th and 13th centuries, as well as the seat of power of a Roman Catholic bishop. Today, it has one of the oldest universities in Europe.

The ancient town of Obidos is a tourist draw.

Farmer with a hoe in the Trás-os-Montes.

Nine months of winter and three months of hell.

—*Local proverb describing the climate in Trás-os-Montes*

THE MOUNTAINS

To the north lies a mountainous region that the Portuguese call the Trás-os-Montes (meaning "Beyond the Mountains"). The mountain ranges there are extensions of the Cantabrian Mountains of northwestern Spain. The winters in the mountains can be fiercely cold, and summer months are hot and dry. Villages in these mountain regions seem as they were in medieval times, and stone milestones provide frequent evidence of Roman occupation. The countryside is rounded with rolling hills and olive groves crowd the riverbanks.

Abundant sources of water have led to the establishment of several hydroelectric dams that have brought growing prosperity to what is still a backward, rural area with poor soil and hardwon crops of rye or potatoes. There are many spas here where visitors "take the cure" from underground mineral waters rich with fluoride and bicarbonate of soda. One of the more popular spas is at Chaves. Amazingly, there are vineyards as well. At the town of Vila Real is an ornate building that serves as the headquarters of the Mateus Rosé wine that is popular worldwide.

The Serra da Estrêla is a great mountain barrier in the center of Portugal. It is the country's tallest chain and contains Estrêla, the nation's highest point at 6,532 feet (1991 m). Corn and rye grow in the valleys of this chain. The villagers weave woolen goods, make sheep's milk cheese, and raise pigs. Covilhã has become a winter sports center, although hiking on trails in the mountains may be an even more popular tourist attraction.

LISBON

Like Rome, the capital city of Lisbon is built on seven hills. It surrounds the natural harbor at the mouth of the Tejo River. Lisbon is sufficiently modern to be chosen as the European City of Culture in 1994. However, it is still decorated with black and white pavements, a Roman tradition that has never been broken. It is dominated by the 10 towers of the Castle of St. George with its Moorish walls. From its restored medieval ramparts there is a view of the Tejo and the great suspension bridge originally called Salazar Bridge but renamed the 25th of April Bridge in honor of the 1974 Revolution. At the heart of the city is the wide piazza, Praça do Comércio, surrounded by 18th-century government buildings.

Further to the west lies Sintra, once the summer palace of the Portuguese kings. The riverside area of Belem is the place where the Portuguese ships once set off to discover the unknown. At this place is the impressive Monastery of Jerónimos, built in memory of explorer Vasco da Gama and his successful journey to India in 1499.

Lisbon's wealth and importance made it a natural choice for the capital when the government was moved from Coimbra in 1298.

ALENTEJO

The spreading plains of central and southern Portugal are called collectively the Alentejo, meaning "Beyond the Tejo River." This area occupies a third of the total land area of Portugal and is covered with fields of wheat, oats, rice, grapes, and tomatoes. Everywhere cork oaks and olive trees grow. The land is dotted with white farmhouses, prehistoric stone circles, and occasional trees, which do not prevent it from grilling to a burnt brown in the hot summer months. The only shade for the sheep and black pigs is provided by the large plantations of cork oaks.

The Alentejo was the heart of Portuguese communism. Great farming estates were taken over by the workers during the 1974 Revolution, but they failed financially from a succession of poor harvests. Now, many of the original owners are buying their land back. They introduce new farming methods that reap better profits, although it is still fairly common for older children to drop out of school to work in the fields.

The main city is Evora, with a population of 45,000. It is an educational and cultural center that is the country's fifth most important town after Lisbon, Oporto, Coimbra, and Guimarães. There are Moorish alleyways, a Roman temple, a Gothic cathedral, and several Renaissance palaces in the city, making it somewhat of a museum town. Traditional crafts include pottery, weaving, and woodcarving.

Crops growing under plastic tents, one of the new farming methods.

ALGARVE

This thin strip of Portugal's southern beaches got its name from the Moorish *al-gharb* (the western land). A local legend tells of a Moorish king who captured a bride from the north. When she pined for the snow of her homeland and became ill, he planted almond trees, and the blossoms both cured her and convinced her of his love.

Long, sandy beaches between rocky coves, together with a rain-free Mediterranean summer climate, has made the Algarve one of the prime tourist destinations of Europe. Situated almost centrally along this southern coastline, the town of Faro acts as a tourist center and airport. The port of Lagos, from which Portuguese fleets used to sail, still has the arcades of its old slave market. To the west are tiny bays, often with eroded rocks and picturesque grottoes. One of the most famous is Praia da Rocha with its weird outcrops of red and yellow sandstone. Past Portimão and Lagos, the beaches become bleaker as far as Sagres, where Prince Henry the Navigator set up his school of navigation.

The Praia da Rocha is famous for its unusual sandstone outcrops.

"Where the land ends and the sea begins..."

—*Luis de Camões in* The Lusiads

Flowers blooming in spring add to the natural beauty of the coastal areas.

FLORA AND FAUNA

Portugal's birdlife is unusually varied because the country is on a main migratory route. Algarve fishers often see dunlins from Iceland, and Alentejo children greet flocks of azure-winged magpies or crested hoopoes. White egrets follow the plough, and storks nest on many a belltower. Golden eagles, falcons, and kestrels hover over the northern mountains. There are even flamingoes on the Tejo estuary.

European field animals, such as rabbits and hares, are common, with a few badgers and foxes. The civet cat still roams, although people often shoot it because it raids poultry yards. In the Peneda-Gerês national park on the far north, there are deer, boar, lynx, and a few remaining wolves, and the nearly extinct Luso-Galician ponies run wild in the park. There are national breeds of dogs: the handsome Serra da Estrêla, the pointer

WATERDOG

This unique breed is a bit like a poodle. It is a large, muscular dog with curly hair (either black and white or brown and white), with webbed feet for better swimming and a tail curved up over its back that serves as a rudder. It can swim as far as five miles, carrying messages between boats, and dive 12 feet deep to pull up fish and nets. Waterdogs bark warnings in a fog and even save men from drowning. They are increasingly rare.

Perdigueiro (once a hunting dog), and the curious waterdog Ceo d'Agua. Madeira claims wildlife fame for its 695 species of beetles!

Portugal's floral kingdom is particularly rich, with over 2,700 specimens of wildflowers. From February to June the southern coastal regions blaze with rock roses, anemones, celandines, thrift, and vetch. The inland scrubland is scented with herbs such as rosemary, thyme, and lavender, and colorful with irises, lupins, and scarlet poppies. Arum lilies grow wild in marshy areas. Flowering rhododendrons and oleander bushes grow in many of the woodlands, and the dark-green, leathery carob bean tree grows in the south. Sweet basil is found everywhere.

"Every traveller passes Madeira at some time or other."

—*Claude Dervenn in* Madeira

PIGS

Wild boar must have been common in primitive Portugal, for the northern villages have many strange pigs carved in granite. Perhaps they had a connection with worship, but today they are part of the menu. The national pig and sausage fair on the south bank of the River Tejo is a vast celebration attracting some 50,000 visitors. The breeders discuss the care of pigs and government regulations regarding slaughtering.

The visitors, however, are more concerned with buying the many varieties of spicy sausages, and feasting on suckling pig or the Alentejo speciality, *pézinhos de coentrada* ("pet-ZEEN-oss da kwen-TRAH-da," or pig trotters flavored with coriander). The pigs of the Alentejo forage each autumn in the orchards of cork trees, stuffing themselves with acorns, herbs, and an occasional truffle. That must provide their special flavor!

THE ISLANDS

Two groups of Atlantic islands, the Azores and Madeira, are Portuguese territory. They are autonomous regions with their own legislatures and governments.

THE AZORES This is a group of nine islands with a total area of 922 square miles (2,388 square km) and a population of 255,000. They lie in the North Atlantic Ocean off the western coast of Africa, about 1,000 miles (1,600 km) from Lisbon. The climate is temperate, with plenty of rain. Volcanic hot springs abound, and extinct craters have created spectacular lakes and bays. Cattle and dairy products, in addition to fishing, support the islanders.

Some say that these islands are the tips of what was once the lost continent of Atlantis, sunk centuries ago by a great volcanic upheaval. There are still earth tremors in the Azores to keep the legend alive, and enough mysterious beauty in the islands to make it seem possible.

MADEIRA Located in the North Atlantic Ocean about 535 miles (856 km) southwest of Lisbon and 350 miles (560 km) off the northwestern coast of Africa, Madeira consists of two large islands and several uninhabited islets with a total area of 314 square miles (813 sq km) and a population of 271,000. It is said that sailors once lit a fire to clear space among its thick forests. The blaze went out of control and burned for seven years. Whether that is true or not, the thick tree growth on the group of islands gave it the name "Madeira," meaning "wood."

Today it has terraced fields climbing up the sheer mountainsides. There is an airport, but visitors can also go by boat and anchor in the offshore water, which is deep enough for cruise liners. Plagued by pirates in the

18th century, disease in its vineyards in the 19th century, and floods and economic slumps more recently, Madeira remains a beautiful place to live.

A certain woman named Miss Phelps took samples of Madeira embroidery to London, and this started a major export industry. The most famous local product is the nutty, spicy Madeira wine. The British ship Bellerophon, carrying Napoleon to exile on Saint Helena, arrived at the capital city of Funchal in 1815. A cask of Madeira wine was put on board to help the defeated emperor forget his sorrow. However, he suffered from indigestion, and the cask was never opened.

Madeira's warm climate is ideal for growing grapes, used to produce a famous sweet red wine called Madeira.

HISTORY

THE PORTUGUESE ARE JUSTLY PROUD of their history. There was a time when Portugal ruled half the known world and its ships carried the most formidable combination of traders and conquerors. That such a past should belong to such a small-sized country is part of the wonder of Portugal.

BEGINNING OF INDEPENDENCE

There are dozens of silent, stonewalled settlements in the northern hills of Portugal. Dating back to almost 1,000 B.C., these were the villages of the Celtic people, who lived as fiercely independent tribes. In the south, Phoenician sailors set up trading stations. They were followed by the Carthaginians from North Africa. The Iberian peninsula later became part of the Roman empire.

Opposite: **Roman mosaic dating back to the second century B.C.**

Above: **Ruins of a Roman temple in Evora built in honor of the goddess Diana.**

Most of Portugal came under the province Romans named Lusitania after a Celtic tribe that had proved tough to subdue. For 400 years, the Romans built roads and bridges, introduced wheat, barley, and grapevines, brought their Latin language and, in the fourth century A.D. introduced Christianity to Portugal. Then barbarian invaders swept through the Roman empire, and in Portugal the Visigoths triumphed.

Sweeping across Arabia and over the hot desert sands of Africa came another religion. In A.D. 711 the Muslim invasion began. The Emir Musa ibn Nusair, Muslim governor of North Africa, invaded the peninsula and killed Rodrigo, the last of the Visigoth kings. Encouraged by this success, he returned two years later with an army of 18,000 men.

The Moors, as they were known, swept through Spain, but chose to settle in the southern part of Portugal where the sunny Algarve region was

Statue of Dom Dinis, a Portuguese king whose reign brought peace and advancement.

much to their liking. It took Portugal five centuries to win it back.

The next 300 years saw constant fighting between Christians and Muslims, until King Afonso of Castile invited Henri of Burgundy to bring his crusaders to assist in forcing back the Moors. As a reward, Henri received Afonso's daughter Teresa and the territory then called *Portucale* ("por-too-KAH-le"). There, their son Afonso Henriques set out to create a kingdom for himself, defeating the forces loyal to his mother. His well-fortified castle at Guimarães became the cradle of modern Portugal.

In 1139 Afonso Henriques claimed to have received a vision of Christ. He believed that the Portuguese were a chosen race. In 1143 Portugal was accepted as a separate kingdom by its neighbors, Castile and León, and four years later Portuguese soldiers seized Lisbon from the Moors.

During years of rival claims to the Portuguese throne, the reign of King Dinis, the poet-king (1279-1325), brought peace, prosperity, and a growth of culture. He had 50 fortresses built along the frontier with Castile, and signed a treaty of friendship with England that was to prove vital in the years ahead.

Powerful Castile cast greedy eyes on Portugal, a country weakened in the 1340s by the plague known as the Black Death. In the decisive battle of Aljubarrota in 1385, King João I, the first in a new line of kings, defeated the Castilians with the aid of archers sent from England, and Portugal's independence was secured.

PORTUGUESE EXPANSION

One man with a vision, known to history as Prince Henry the Navigator, spurred Portugal on to become the most powerful nation on earth in the 16th century. It first colonized Madeira and the Azores, then explored the west coast of Africa, discovering the Cape Verde Islands and the Gulf of Guinea. In 1487 Bartolomeu Dias rounded the Cape of Good Hope.

When Christopher Columbus, sailing under the Spanish flag, went west and discovered the American continents, the pope ruled that the unknown world was to be divided between Spain and Portugal. Spain was to have the lands west of an imaginary line west of the Cape Verde Islands, while Portugal might have the undiscovered world east of that line—an empire that was to include Brazil, and Macau on the Chinese coast.

Portuguese exploration continued, and they were the first Westerners in Ceylon, Sumatra, Malacca, Timor, and the Moluccas, and the first Europeans to trade with China and Japan and to see Australia. Although the Portuguese caravels led by Vasco da Gama had sailed as far as India in 1498, it was Portuguese navigator Ferdinand Magellan (whose voyage was sponsored by Spain) who first circumnavigated the globe.

Vasco da Gama presenting himself at the Indian royal court in 1498 (from a 19th century engraving).

PRINCE HENRY THE NAVIGATOR

The fourth son of King João I headed the inspiration that sent Portuguese ships probing the furthest seas of the world. On the rocky peninsula of Sagres in the Algarve, where he lived as austerely as a monk, he founded a school of navigation. In the company of navigators, mapmakers, and astronomers, his greatest objective was to find a sea route from Europe to the East. His team of experts improved the instruments of navigation, taught sailors to find their position by the stars, and redesigned the caravel (a speedy 60-foot ship) so it could sail against the wind.

The earliest voyages to Madeira and Cape Bojador, south of the Canary Islands, were financed by the prince himself. Later, societies were formed to send Portuguese expeditions ever further, yet these returned richer in knowledge than wealth.

The Monument to the Discoveries at Belem (toward the seaward side of Lisbon) was erected to mark the 500th anniversary of the death of Prince Henry. It is in the stylized shape of a caravel, bearing 33 human figures representing people linked with the voyages of Portuguese discoveries, and Prince Henry is at the front of them all.

"There is no peril so great that the hope of reward will not make it greater."

–attributed to Prince Henry the Navigator

RESTORATION OF INDEPENDENCE

In 1580, King Philip II of Spain swept in to annex Portugal, whose army had been destroyed by Moroccan invaders. It was not until 60 years later, on December 1, 1640 (now a national holiday), that Spanish rule was overthrown by plotters on behalf of the Duke of Bragança, who became King João IV. His daughter married King Charles II of England, and the marriage brought a gift to Portugal of 10 warships and two regiments each of cavalry and infantry, which helped defeat Spanish attempts to recapture Portugal.

The discovery of gold and diamonds in the Portuguese colony of Brazil brought new wealth and a restructured economy to Lisbon. King João V embarked on several ambitious projects, although the power of the monarchy was increasingly questioned by the people and threatened by the church. The king made his own decisions and seldom called his *cortes* ("kor-TEZ," or parliament) to meet. He was succeeded by his son, José I, who did not share his father's passion for power, and who left the job of ruling Portugal to his secretary, the Marquis de Pombal, under whom Portugal's trade in port wine, sugar and tobacco flourished. The tax system was improved.

Then disaster struck on the morning of All Saints Day, November 1, 1755. Lisbon was hit by a massive earthquake. Buildings collapsed, fires raged, and 30,000 people died. But even this did not daunt Pombal, who set about rebuilding the city. In tackling his country's problems, Pombal made many enemies. Despite advances such as a new economic stability, the banning of slavery, and the reformation of Coimbra University, Pombal was dismissed when José I died in 1777.

In 1793, the French general Napoleon invaded Portugal, which had taken sides with Britain against France. Although British troops were sent to help, the Portuguese royal family fled to Brazil. After the battle of Buçaco in which the French lost 5,000 troops, the British general Wellington withdrew his forces behind the Torres Vedras lines, which had been built to defend Lisbon, and the French troops eventually retreated as well. In 1815, Wellington defeated Napoleon in a final battle at Waterloo in Belgium. King João VI returned after 14 years in Brazil to a wild welcome from the population.

Founded in Lisbon in 1290, Coimbra University moved in the 1500s to its present site, a royal palace that once belonged to King João III.

Dom Miguel tried to seize the throne in 1826 but was defeated and exiled.

CONSTITUTIONAL MONARCHY

A new constitution was drawn up in 1822, putting an end to the traditional powers of the monarchy. Meanwhile, King João VI, who in 1816 had become king of Portugal while living in Brazil, accepted the terms of the new constitution and returned to his homeland in 1821. He left his son, Dom Pedro, in charge of Brazil. After his father's death in 1826, Dom Pedro returned to Portugal because his uncle Dom Miguel had ignored the new constitution and seized the throne. He defeated Miguel in battle but died soon afterward in 1834, plunging his country into 50 years of political unrest.

Two political groups vied for power: conservatives wanted Portugal to regain its financial strength; progressives wanted more voting rights and less power in the hands of the government. Meanwhile Portugal was virtually bankrupt and heavily in debt, with the largest amount owed to Britain, then the world's most powerful trading nation. Both countries ruled over colonies in Africa, but Portugal was forced by Britain to forget her dreams of uniting Portuguese Southwest Africa (now Namibia) and Portuguese East Africa (now Mozambique) into an African empire. In 1892 the Portuguese government declared itself bankrupt, and the land emptied of people. They emigrated at a rate of 40,000 per year to Brazil, the colonies, and the United States.

Feeling that the king had allowed the honor of Portugal to be stained, the newly formed Republican party urged that Portugal should become a republic, with elected government officials. King Carlos I appointed a reformist, João Franco, as premier. To impose his unpopular reforms, Franco dismissed parliament and threw his political opponents into jail or had them deported. In retaliation, the Republicans launched a military takeover in 1908. The coup failed, and the royal government reacted harshly. During the accompanying violence, King Carlos I and his heir were assassinated. It was believed that the assassination was unintentional and that the target had been the hated Franco.

King Carlos I's successor, King Manuel II, was received sympathetically, but unstable conditions prevented him from carrying out his duties. Before long, revolution was in the air. On October 4, 1910, Republican ships sailed up the Tejo to Lisbon. They bombarded the palace, while sympathetic troops and civilians held the Rotunda. King Manuel II sailed off on his royal yacht into exile in England. The Portuguese republic was born.

THE FIRST REPUBLIC

During the 16 years from 1910 to 1926, Portuguese politics resulted in 45 changes of government. The changes were effected by military power, since neither the president nor the prime minister of the newly constituted republic had been given the power to dissolve parliament. When World War I (1914-18) broke out, Britain was short of ships and asked Portugal for assistance. So in February 1916 Portugal seized German ships sheltering in what had been, until then, neutral Portuguese ports. Having entered the war on the Allied side, Portugal defended its African colonies of Angola and Mozambique against German attacks. As social unrest increased at home, a military takeover in 1926 met no armed opposition.

"I am Portuguese and will be always. I believe I have done my duty as king in all circumstances."

—Portugal's last king, known as "Manuel the Unfortunate"

In 1926 the military seized power and chose General Oscar Carmona as president.

THE SECOND REPUBLIC

General Oscar Carmona was declared president of Portugal by the military powers in 1926, but it was the minister of finance, António de Oliveira Salazar, who was to become the real ruler of the country.

Salazar became prime minister in 1932, and the following year, a new constitution of 1933 proclaimed the *Estado Novo* ("es-TA-do NOH-vo," or New State) in which the power of the state was increased and political parties were replaced by the National Union.

Salazar had complete control over the country's finances and his strict budget controls and reformed taxation brought financial stability. A countrywide improvement of roads, harbors, airports, and hospitals began. Dams and bridges were built, and agricultural methods were updated.

However, he ruled as a dictator and set up a secret police force that eliminated all opposition to his government. Tight censorship prevented anti-Salazar views from reaching the public. Some political groups were outlawed, and their members were harassed by the secret police.

When World War II (1939-45) broke out, Salazar succeeded in keeping Portugal neutral, although he had signed a treaty of friendship with General Franco of Spain that the two nations would consult together to safeguard their independence. Salazar also allowed Britain to build military bases on the Azores.

The Portuguese people were violently anti-Nazi, shouting and drumming their boots on the floor whenever Hitler appeared in film newsreels. Portugal became a safe destination for political and religious refugees fleeing Nazi Germany. At the end of the war, Portugal joyously celebrated the Allied victory. Salazar refused to allow Angola, Mozambique, or Guinea-Bissau to become independent, although in 1961 Portugal was unable to prevent India from seizing Goa.

In the presidential election of 1958, General Humberto Delgado, who expressed firm opposition to Salazar, was the popular candidate for the presidency. He was defeated by the official candidate in what many claimed was electoral fraud. Delgado went into exile, where he was murdered in 1965 by agents apparently from the Portuguese secret police.

"We do not ask for much. An understanding and consciousness of the fatherland and of national unity; of the family, the primary social unit; of authority and obedience to authority..."

—Antonio Salazar, outlining the ideals of his New State

Hitler's troops during World War II, when Portugal became a safe destination for political and religious refugees fleeing the persecutions of Nazi Germany.

ANTÓNIO DE OLIVEIRA SALAZAR

Prime minister of Portugal from 1932 to 1968, Salazar was a quiet professor of economics from Coimbra University who achieved what seemed an impossible task: that of rebuilding Portugal into a country with a firm government and a reliable economy.

From a skilled economist admired for his honesty and genius, Salazar became a relentless, autocratic dictator during the 36 years of his rule. He showed his authoritarian ways in his complete control of government and departmental expenditure. Nothing was to be spent without his approval. In his manipulation of politics, there was no open debate. Ministers were rarely called to any council meeting. Deeply influenced by the ideology

and inquisitorial methods of fascism, he admired Hitler's Gestapo and started a youth brigade compulsory for all between the ages of 11 and 14. It used the Nazi salute and was modeled on the Hitler Youth group.

In August 1968, Salazar fell from his chair onto a tiled floor. He was taken to a hospital where an operation on his brain was successful, but he subsequently died on July 27, 1970. To the end, the dictator believed that he had kept Portugal "proudly alone."

THE THIRD REPUBLIC

After Salazar's death, Dr. Marcello Caetano, a member of Salazar's government, became prime minister. He tried to introduce economic and political reforms, but his half-hearted efforts were not popular. Once again, military forces struggled to take power, until a revolution succeeded in April 1974.

General Antonio de Spinola did not take part in the bloodless military coup that accepted the unconditional surrender of Caetano and his government, but he benefited from it. He was inaugurated as president, and his new government made banks, large farms, and other industries the property of the state. There were strikes and a shortage of bread, and public transport was in disarray. His government did not last and over the next two years, six provisional governments came and went. Civil wars had erupted in the colonies that had suddenly been given independence, and this time Portuguese refugees fled back to their homeland.

In April 1975, 91% of all registered voters voted in an election that saw the Socialist Party of Dr. Mario Soares win with a slight majority. In due course, he was appointed prime minister, but no party had an overall majority until July 1987. In that year, Anibal Cavaco Silva's Social Democrats were voted in with 50.15% of the votes. Soares had been elected president the year before and proved a highly popular nonparty leader who won re-election by a landslide in 1992.

Portugal joined the European Community in 1986 as its poorest member. This group, to which most western European countries belong, follows economic policies that benefit all of its members. Portugal joined in the hope that membership would ease its economic hardships.

Dr. Mario Soares is now in his second term as the country's president.

The country's close ties with Great Britain continue. Queen Elizabeth II has visited the country twice, and in 1987 Prince Charles and Princess Diana's royal tour did the double duty of promoting British trade and celebrating the 600th anniversary of the wedding of King João I to his English bride Philippa.

GOVERNMENT

PORTUGAL HAS STRUGGLED ITS WAY through the domination of invading powers, absolute monarchy, shaky republics, dictatorship, and revolutions to arrive at today's democracy. As a result, its people largely distrust the government and retain a desire to have a royal family once more.

CONSTITUTION

It was not until 1976 that the Portuguese people enjoyed a constitution that allowed them majority rule by a democratically elected government. Progress toward becoming a republic began with the overthrow of the monarchy in October 1910.

During the next 16 years Portugal was ruled by no fewer than 45 governments. Under the First Republic (1910-1926), new laws created a

"Portugal ... had three revolutions and four changes of government in one day."

—Will Rogers writing in 1926

Opposite: **Many government offices are housed in the Praça do Comércio, a square in Lisbon .**

Left: **Elected members of Portugal's National Assembly meet in the ornate parliamentary building in Lisbon.**

Since Anibal Cavaco Silva became prime minister in 1987, his government has been returning some state-run farmland and businesses to private ownership.

two-chambered parliament with a president, abolished noble titles, and changed the national coinage from the *real* ("RAY-al," meaning royal) to the *escudo* ("ess-KOO-do," meaning shield). The Second Republic (1926-1974) was a republic in name only, as Portugal was ruled for most of that time by Salazar. It was the Third Republic that saw the introduction of the present constitution on April 2, 1976.

A revised constitution (replacing that of 1976) was approved on August 12, 1982. This abolished the military Council of the Revolution and reduced the role of the president, who can now be elected for a maximum of two five-year terms of office. In turn, the president appoints a prime minister and a council of ministers.

There is a 230-member National Assembly elected for a four-year term (reduced from 250 at the 1991 election). In June 1989, parliament approved further reforms that replaced the socialist economy with more democratic methods. In the election of January 1991, Dr. Soares was elected for his second term as president.

It is interesting to note that the 1974 Revolution that brought the years of dictatorship (under Salazar and his successor Caetano) to an end came from the south of Portugal, where rich landowners wanted their share of running the country, whereas the changes introduced in the 1980s came from the north, where more conservative-minded owners of small properties were wary of change.

Today, the only remains of the Portuguese empire are the autonomous regions of the Azores and Madeira. Both these groups of islands have their own locally elected governments, but their general laws fall under Portugal's constitution.

MACAU

The Macau peninsula at the mouth of the Pearl River in China has been a Portuguese colony since 1557.

Constant ferryloads of visitors come from Hong Kong on the opposite bank, for tourism is a major industry. Many of them come for round-the-clock gambling at the seven casinos in this "Las Vegas of the East." There are two racetracks, one for horses, one for greyhounds; and an annual Grand Prix on the roads. For centuries, people have visited the ancient Temple of the Goddess A-Ma, the patron goddess of fishers, a temple that was already there when Portugal took possession of the colony.

Macau consists of the picturesque old city of Santa Nome de Deus de Macau with its modern skyscraper waterfront and the islands of Taipa and Colôane, linked to the mainland by causeways. The official language is Portuguese, but most people speak the local Cantonese dialect. By an agreement made in 1974, Macau is a Chinese territory under Portuguese administration, with administrative and economic autonomy. It is scheduled to be handed over to China in 1999.

POLITICAL PARTIES

At present there are some 26 political parties in Portugal. In most elections in recent years, no party has held an overall majority, so coalition between parties was essential. However, in the 1991 election the Social Democratic Party won an absolute majority in the Assembly with 50% of the vote (135 seats). The present government is headed by Anibal Cavaco Silva, leader of the Social Democrats. The government has been busy privatizing everything that had been nationalized after the revolution. The gap between rich and poor has not narrowed.

The Assembly has a maximum of 250 members, elected by 20 constituencies on a system of proportional representation. All Portuguese over 18 years of age have a vote.

Police guard in ceremonial dress.

NATIONAL DEFENSE

Portugal is defended by armed forces totaling around 61,800. About half of these are drafted, through a program of compulsory military service that used to last 12–15 months. In 1991, this was reduced to 4–8 months for the army, and 4–18 months for the navy and air force. Those with valid reasons for avoiding military service are allowed to perform an alternative community service.

Although soldiers in uniform are a fairly common sight, the defense budget is relatively small. The army consists of conventional troops, plus the paramilitary National Republican Guard, Public Security Police, and Border Guard. In June 1993, the total strength of the armed forces was about 100,000.

The navy is divided into three commands: Lisbon and Portimão (for the mainland coastline), the Azores, and Madeira. Its more publicized activities are sea rescues. Portugal also has an air force equipped with combat, training, and transport aircraft.

Lisbon is the naval base of the North Atlantic Treaty Organization (NATO) Iberian Atlantic Command. In 1993, there were 1,500 U.S. troops stationed in Portugal, mainly at the air force base at Lajes in the Azores.

FOREIGN POLICY

Portugal joined the European Community on January 1, 1986, a move that has done much to help the country's economy. Despite centuries of distrust, in their first years of membership Portugal and Spain decided to be friends and abolished border controls. Since then, trade, investment, and tourism between the two countries have increased. Together, the two Iberian nations now have a stronger voice in European politics than either of them would have alone.

Portugal is also a member of the United Nations, NATO, and the Council of Europe—and took its turn as president of the European Community in 1992. Both Portugal and Spain were admitted to the European Union in 1988.

Strong cultural ties are maintained with other Portuguese-speaking countries, such as Angola, the Cape Verde Islands, Guinea-Bissau, Mozambique, and São Tomé and Principe. From its historical ties, Portugal tries to maintain an even warmer relationship with Brazil.

Portugal's "oldest ally" (as Winston Churchill called the relationship) is Great Britain. The Treaty of Windsor in 1385 declared perpetual peace and friendship, followed by the Methuen Treaty of 1703, establishing the longest-standing international friendship of modern times. Among its terms is the provision that Portuguese wines would be admitted to Britain at a third less duty than that payable on French wines "forever."

During World War I, Portugal answered Britain's request for assistance by seizing German ships sheltering in its ports. Then in World War II, the Portuguese government gave Britain permission to build military bases on the Azores from which to attack German submaries in the Atlantic. As recently at the Falklands War, the British were once again allowed to use the Azores as a base for navy operations.

"It's not exactly the Portugal we dreamed about."

—Col. Vitor Alves, one of those who launched the 1974 Revolution

Evora is one of four judicial districts. The city is also regarded as an educational and cultural center.

JUSTICE AND ADMINISTRATION

Mainland Portugal is divided into 18 administrative districts (plus three in the Azores and one in Madeira), each with its own elected civil governor. Local administration is handled by municipal authorities in the towns and by parish assemblies in the villages.

The courts of justice are headed by the Constitutional Court and the Supreme Court of Justice in Lisbon. Under these are other judicial, administrative, tax, and military courts. They are divided into four judicial districts: Lisbon, Oporto, Coimbra, and Evora. Each district has four courts of appeal. A tribunal checks new laws to ensure they agree with the terms of the constitution. As long ago as 1867, the death penalty for civil crimes was abolished.

The police are formed in two bodies: the Public Security Police, who maintain general public order and look after the city traffic; and the National Republican Guard, which supplies armed police in rural areas, as well as traffic officers countrywide. Pickpockets do exist where there are large crowds and on the Lisbon subway, and increasing poverty in the swelling urban areas is already creating a disturbing increase in crime, mostly theft—to eat or to stay alive. Drug dealing is also evident, and the resources of the antidrug squad are strained. Yet President Soares is able to walk among his people without the need for a bodyguard.

Traditionally, Portugal is divided into 11 provinces. They are the Minho, Trás-os-Montes, Douro Litoral, Beira Alta, Beira Litoral, Beira Baixa, Estremadura, Ribatejo, Alto Alentejo, Baixo Alentejo, and Algarve. Although these have not been official since 1959, most Portuguese still refer to these geographical regions in the old way.

THE PORTUGUESE FLAG

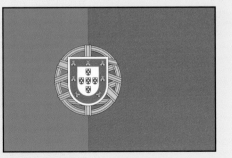

In the center of the flag are five small, blue shields, each bearing five white discs. Dating from 1139, these represent Christian victories over the Moors. The red border contains seven yellow castles and is known as the "Bordure of Castile," commemorating King Alfonso III's marriage to Beatrice of Castile in 1252. The yellow sphere behind it is an old navigational instrument, a reminder of the country's seafaring tradition. All these stand on a red and green background, the red almost twice as wide as the green. The green represents hope, and the red is symbolic of the blood shed during the 1910 revolution that brought about the republic.

ECONOMY

AS A RELATIVELY SMALL AND RURAL COUNTRY, Portugal used to survive on farming and reselling imports from its dwindling colonies. In the 1970s, two loans had to be negotiated with the International Monetary Fund. The country's economy plunged further in 1984, bringing with it an inflation rate of 29%.

Industrial progress was only possible when a change to the constitution in 1989 enabled state-run companies to be sold off. Private enterprise began to modernize both the economy and society, but many small businesses choked to death in a bureaucratic system of licenses and permits. Banks and insurance companies were nationalized in 1975 but are now being privatized again. From 1984, new private banks have been allowed to operate.

In 1984 Portugal was Europe's poorest country, but since it joined the European Community in 1986 its economy has strengthened. Using massive financial aid, Portugal has built new roads and business blocks. Most Portuguese look around with pride at their growing country and wonder why there are still traffic jams and too few telephones.

The Portuguese unit of money is the *escudo* ("ess-KOO-do") which is divided into 100 *centavos* ("sen-TAH-vose"). When written, the *escudos* are put on the left of the $ sign and *centavos* on the right; so 3 *escudos* and 50 *centavos* is written 3$50. A thousand *escudos* (1,000$00) is often referred to as a *conta* ("KON-ta"). A few years ago, there was a shortage of small coins in Portugal. In many places people used sweets or stamps instead of coinage.

Opposite: **Marble is quarried for local construction.**

Above: **The Portuguese unit of money is the *escudo*, divided into 100 *centavos*.**

AGRICULTURE AND FORESTRY

Portugal is a land of fruit, wine, and trees. The majority of its population is engaged in some form of agriculture. Small farms owned by individual families occupy about a quarter of the cultivated land. Grapes (for table grapes and wine) are grown almost everywhere, as are olives. Cereal crops are oats and rice. Apples, pears, oranges, and peaches are grown for export. Tomatoes, for processing into tomato paste, are another cash crop. Portugal does not grow enough food for itself, so wheat, corn, and meat have to be imported.

About a quarter of the country is covered by forest, mostly pine (for timber or resin) or eucalyptus (for paper pulp) plantations. Portugal is the world's major producer of cork (176,000 tons in 1989), coming from some 500,000 acres of cork forests in the Alentejo and Algarve. Besides providing corks for Portugal's wines, the cork is used for insulation, fishing floats, tiles, soundproofing, and such sporting essentials as table-tennis bats and badminton shuttlecocks. The cork trade brings Portugal more than $200 million a year in exports. Although profitable, it is a slow moneymaker. By law, cork bark may only be stripped from a tree once every 11 years.

About one-fifth of the total work force is occupied on the land, in some places still using out-of-date farming methods. Profits are persistently declining. Experts have advised that an increase in the country's forested areas of pine and eucalyptus would bring valuable economic rewards, and recent years have seen considerable reforestation.

Cork oak trees flourish in the south. Their bark provides cork, the raw material for 80% of the bottle stoppers used around the world.

HOME OF THE PORT WINE

Portugal is the world's sixth largest wine producer. Its most famous vineyards are located in the Douro valley, where the rich, red port wine is produced. (The wine takes its name from the exporting harbor of Oporto). The hillsides are exposed to scorching heat in summer and crisp frost in winter, which combine to produce wine of excellent quality. The country's other famous wine is the *vinho verde* ("VEEN-yo VAIR-di," or young, green wine) from the northwest, an excellent accompaniment to the country's many fish dishes. Also famous are the nutty, strong-tasting wines from the volcanic island of Madeira.

INDUSTRY

Portugal possesses considerable natural wealth but is only moderately industrialized. This is now one of the economic areas of the country that is expanding rapidly. Many industries were taken over by the government in 1974, and many still remain state-owned. The main items produced are: textiles and clothing (nearly a third of all exports), canned sardines, tuna, tomato concentrate, cement, paper pulp, fertilizers, and refined olive oil. Power is provided by impressive hydroelectric operations in the northern mountains.

There are minerals in Portugal, but no sources of oil or gas, and coal is scarce. Iron and tin deposits are worked in the north, as well as wolframite, a hard mineral used in making tungsten for electrical equipment. There are large reserves of uranium and a little gold. Limestone, granite, and good quality marble are quarried for local building. There is a modern steelworks, and two large shipbuilding and repair yards are located in Lisbon and Setúbal.

Sardine fleet at Portimão. About half of Portugal's sardine catch is canned for export.

FISHING

The area in which the Portuguese are able to fish (their territorial waters) is 20 times greater than the land of Portugal itself. This includes 525 miles (845 km) of coastline, plus the islands of Madeira and the Azores. Fishing, therefore, was of tremendous economic importance until the 1960s, when the sardines (vital to Portugal's canning industry) began to deplete. Since then, with dwindling profits, little has been done to update the fishing fleet. Over half are more than 20 years old, and 85% are small fishing boats of under 5 tons in weight.

Today, the bulk of the catch is still sardines, with cod and tuna and some lobster and shellfish. The wooden-hulled boats with high, broad bows, called *traineiras* ("tray-NEY-ras"), are painted in bright colors. This enables fishers to recognize individual boats at a distance.

Today, with loans from the European Community, money is being spent on better boats and equipment, for fishing provides work for some 40,000 people and also contributes about 30% of the national consumption of animal protein. The fishing industry cannot supply local needs, and about a quarter of the fish eaten have to be imported.

TOURISM

Cheaper prices and sunny beaches have made Portugal (especially the picturesque Algarve coast) into an increasingly popular tourist venue. Some 18 million tourists bring in about two billion U.S. dollars in foreign revenue each year. Looking ahead, EXPO '98 will be held in Lisbon, when around nine million visitors are expected over a three-month period to explore the exhibits on the theme, *The Oceans, a Legacy for the Future.*

Portugal has been quick to realize the possibilities of attracting tourists. In addition to 1,700 hotels around the country, it has converted many historic palaces, convents, and castles into *pousadas* where visitors can sample hospitality of a more traditional and gracious style. There are also youth hostels, camping parks, and simple accommodations offered in farms and private houses.

The Algarve, with its springtime almond blossoms, golden beaches, and blue summer seas, has a wealth of tourist activities—from walking trails to international golf, inland drives to medieval castles or Roman ruins. The harsh hills of the Trás-os-Montes, with their natural forests and terraced vineyards, are now being discovered by tourists as well.

Estoril's casino, restaurants, hotels, and fine beaches make it a major tourist destination.

Footwear is one of Portugal's leading manufactured items.

TRADE AND INVESTMENT

Trade has been in the Portuguese blood for many centuries. As the country's sailors discovered fresh lands in Africa, so its traders arrived with food crops, fine horses, and sharp weapons. In exchange, they took away gold, ivory, and slaves.

Today, most trading is done with European Community members. Border controls with Spain and some other countries have been abolished. Nearly half of Portugal's food is imported from fellow European countries. The major imports are cereals, meat, machinery, industrial equipment, crude oil, and motor vehicles. Major exports include cork, timber, paper pulp, canned fish, wine, textiles, and footwear.

Trade clearly exhibits the deficiencies of the Portuguese economy. Imports are higher than exports. The increased wages negotiated by Portuguese trade unions (with only slight improvements in industrial efficiency) have pushed up production costs, so Portuguese products are not sufficiently competitive with those from other European countries.

Outside of Europe, Portugal is building strong financial contacts with the United States and Japan. Trade with Japan began as long ago as 1543, when firearms were introduced to that country in exchange for silver. Now Japanese investment is welcomed in Portugal. Mitsubishi has invested in acrylics; Aoki has bought property in Lisbon; and Nissho Iwai has built a factory to manufacture jeeps and commercial vehicles.

EMPLOYMENT

Portuguese workers are given social security and unemployment benefits in return for a social tax (in 1992) of 11% on wages paid by the employee and 24% paid by the employer. According to official figures, unemployment in 1990 was only five percent. (Some say the government keeps these figures low by including training programs as "employment.")

An agreement between trade unions, employees, and the government in 1991 involved a voluntary wage ceiling, a commitment to labor peace, improvements in working conditions, and 15% increases in pension and social security payments. The per capita income has risen from $1,200 in 1974, to $2,100 in 1985, and over $5,000 in 1990. Yet Portugal remains one of the poorest nations in Europe.

Back in the 1940s, workers were forbidden to strike, but all that changed with the 1974 Revolution. Legal trade unions brought with them a constant wave of strikes for fairer employment practices. Today, there are two large trade unions for workers: *Intersindical,* which is communist controlled; and the democratically run *União Geral de Trabalhadores.*

Grape harvest in the Minho, where farm workers pluck the fruit by hand.

The government is now trying to upgrade agriculture, industry, and public services such as the telephone and transport systems. These activities have traditionally needed many workers. After modernization is in place, higher unemployment may result because machines will replace some forms of manual labor, but this is a short-term problem as the country pushes ahead into the 21st century.

TRANSPORTATION

In Portugal, the smaller roads are narrow and bumpy, and the highway system is still being built in places. Many prefer to travel by the economical train service despite the lines for tickets. A few *rapidos* ("RAP-ee-dos") provide fast luxury travel between major towns.

Officially, Portugal has 5,830 miles (9,328 km) of national roads, 1,910 miles (3,056 km) of rail track, subway and tramway systems in Lisbon, and a tramway in Oporto. A superhighway has been completed between Lisbon and Oporto, cutting driving time to just over three hours.

Once a proud sailing nation, Portugal no longer has a great fleet, although Lisbon and Oporto remain busy commercial ports. Portline is a state-owned company that operates commercial transport, mostly between Portugal and northern Europe or Portuguese-speaking countries in Africa. TAP (Air Portugal) has been operating for over 40 years and flies to 24 countries. There are international airports in Lisbon, Oporto, and Faro (in the Algarve), and in the Azores and Madeira.

THE FUTURE

Isolated from Europe through many centuries (often by choice), Portugal has taken a big step forward by joining the European Community. Greater unemployment and higher prices may well be inevitable as the country works at modernizing its economy and privatizing areas taken over by the government in earlier years. In 1993, the economy entered a recession and the *escudo* was devalued by 6.5% that year. Foreign investment declined sharply. The 1994 budget, however, aimed to encourage foreign investment and to promote recovery. The Gross Domestic Product contracted by one percent in 1993 but a growth rate of 0.5% was envisaged for 1994. Today, Portugal is more economically optimistic than it has been for many years.

"Driving examiners went on strike, surprising many of us who had doubted their existence."

—*Marion Kaplan, in* The Portuguese

Amoreiras Shopping Center, a futuristic-looking building complex.

PORTUGUESE

THE WARLIKE CELTS came from the Alps and the Danube basin, and their wandering tribes spread over much of western Europe, including Britain and Ireland. They arrived on the Iberian peninsula around 700 B.C., where they intermarried with the local Iberians. Many Celtic hilltop villages can still be seen in northern Portugal.

When Greek and Phoenician traders sailed into such natural harbors as the Tejo estuary, they met the powerful Lusitani tribe (of Celtic and Iberian origins). Then, in 210 B.C., the Roman empire brought its *pax Romana* ("pax ro-MAH-na," or the Roman peace)—resisted by the Lusitanians for some 50 years. (The Alentejo town of Beja was once named Pax Julia after peace was made there by Julius Caesar with the Lusitani.) In the fifth century A.D., Roman power lost out to successive invasions of Germanic peoples. The Swabians and Visigoths reached Portugal, and their fair hair and blue eyes can still be seen among the people of the Minho and Trás-os-Montes.

Spain and Portugal were invaded by the Moors and Arabs in the eighth century, and their darker features (and distinctive architecture) can still be seen in Portugal's southern lands. Most Portuguese today have the common Mediterranean characteristics of brown or black hair and brown eyes.

Over the last two centuries, many Portuguese have emigrated to Brazil, Europe, or the United States to seek better conditions. Thus, despite a high birth rate, the population has grown slowly. Since the 1970s, however, the number of Portuguese emigrants has declined, and Portugal has more than 10 million inhabitants today.

Opposite and below: **The Portuguese have had a rich history, resulting in mixed ancestry and features.**

Men relaxing along the Esplanade in Lagos.

CHARACTER

Portuguese ways are a mixture of old and new. They cling to superstitious traditions, yet are proud of the changes taking place around them. The warmth of the Mediterranean blends with the tough challenge of the Atlantic. There seems only one common characteristic: time, for all Portuguese, is unimportant. No one is ever in a hurry.

Staunchly Christian, the Portuguese are openly hospitable. They quarrel loudly, make friends again swiftly, and welcome visitors with great courtesy. Talking is one of the national pleasures: across the seats of a bus, out of the window to passersby, or wobbling along on a bicycle over cobblestones. But the Portuguese are not much concerned with matters beyond Portuguese borders. To survive on the year's harvest or celebrate in better times—these are more important than the broader vision of the European Community. Above all, the Portuguese have been independent throughout most of their long history. They intend to keep things that way.

WHERE ONE LIVES MAKES A DIFFERENCE

The population density is higher in the north than in the south (apart from the overpopulated Algarve coast) and more concentrated along the coast than inland. As with other countries worldwide, there is a steady trickle of urbanization: young people eager to make their way up in the world leave their rural upbringing for hopefully better jobs in the urban sprawls around Lisbon and Oporto, where about 75% of the active workforce in industry is situated.

Farm workers in the south washing turnips in a stream.

In a land of sunbaked plains, remote mountain villages, industrial harbors, and tourist-filled beaches, it is hardly surprising to find regional differences in the ways the Portuguese live. Until the 12th century, Portugal was one of the medieval kingdoms of Spain. It is still a land split apart by mountain ranges. Each region has its own traditions.

In the northern Trás-os-Montes, the village folk are poor but self-sufficient, living a communal life that has not changed for centuries. In Monsanto, there are houses carved out of solid granite rock. Ox-carts run on wooden wheels and oxen can be seen hauling a handheld plough. In the Minho, the harvest festival is a celebration of songs, dances, and drink.

In the southern regions of the Algarve and Alentejo, the Moorish legacy is evident. The people say that one sign of their Arab blood is the way they cherish water and trees. They have another characteristic: while most Portuguese are not renowned for tidiness, the Alentejanos are an exception. Their old walled towns are litter-free.

"It's not quite Portuguese to be just Portuguese."

—*Fernando Pessoa, Portuguese poet*

PORTUGUESE JEWS

Jewish families have lived in Portugal for over 1,000 years. They first settled in the country around the eighth century, during the time of the Moors. In 1446, a royal ordinance decreed that the Jews had to live in segregated Jewish quarters called Judiaria. Compared to other European countries of the time, however, Portugal was considered a relatively safe place for the Jews to live and work in. In time, they came to wield considerable power as doctors, financiers, astrologers, printers, and the world's finest mapmakers.

In 1492, in the course of religious persecution, Spain expelled its Jews and about 60,000 fled to Portugal. They settled in Guarda, Belmonte, Tomar, Bragança, and Viana do Castelo. Four years later, however, the santuary offered to them in Portugal was repealed. In an attempt to retain their financial expertise at a time of burgeoning wealth, they were offered the option of being baptized as "New Christians." Many refused and were seized and burned, while others escaped to Morocco, Brazil, and the Netherlands, or to start the first Jewish community in New York. Others stayed on and continued to exercise their faith in secret as "Hidden Jews."

Today, small groups of Portuguese Jews remain, still clinging to their Jewish origins. Curiously, all their family names mean a plant, animal, or bird. Many Portuguese probably have some Jewish blood following centuries of intermarriage.

INFLUENCE OF THE SEA

The sea has always been the greatest influence on the Portuguese as a people. They think of themselves as a seafaring race, sturdily proud of such explorers as Dias and da Gama. The Atlantic governs their weather and the fish harvest; the Mediterranean brings the tourists.

Fishers with brightly painted boats at Lagos.

For years, some of the fishing boats would set sail from Lisbon for the Grand Banks off Newfoundland. With them they took dories (one-man fishing boats) in which fishers went out alone to fish for cod. They then brought their catch back to the mother ship to be salted and stored. After six months, they returned to Portugal, where the fish was sundried. Such old fishing styles have not totally died out.

The fishers of the Atlantic coast seem a breed of their own. While tourists gaze at the brightly painted boats or shelter in striped tents along Nazaré's mile-long bay, the weather-beaten fisherfolk face the storms of the chill Atlantic, day after day, for what may be a handful of sardines.

Their boats, once launched over log rollers and pulled ashore by yoked oxen, may now have slipways and motorized hoists. That does not make fishing any less dangerous. Fishers and their families tend to face the future one day at a time. The fatalistic acceptance that sailors' families develop of the dangers of the sea are echoed in the sad singing of the *fadista* ("fa-DIS-ta"), or folksinger.

A LAND OF EMIGRATION

With the blood of the ancient explorers in their veins, the Portuguese have seldom hesitated to sail off to find fortune in some distant land. The first great gold rush was to Brazil. Whole families emigrated, crammed into packed boats. Between 1886 and 1926, over a million people left Portugal, driven out increasingly by poverty and civil war at home. Another million left during the dictatorship of Salazar. It is estimated that there are some four million Portuguese abroad. Many are in the United States; perhaps 50,000 in Australia; some 650,000 in South Africa; well over a million in Brazil; and 160,000 in Venezuela. They still emigrate nowadays: many go north to France (about 5,000 a year), and it is said that Paris has the largest Portuguese population of any city after Lisbon. Others go to the United States (about 2,000 a year) or to the many Portuguese-speaking countries.

But there are also the *retornados* ("re-tor-NAH-dose")—those forced to return, like the 700,000 refugees from war-torn Angola and Mozambique. Some bring back skills with them and new ideas to challenge the old traditions at home, others bring only poverty to a country that already has enough. Over 100,000 returned in 1990, including 45,000 from Africa, 11,000 from Brazil, 8,000 from the United Kingdom, and 7,000 from the United States.

Gold washing in Brazil, where hordes of people flocked in search of fortune.

TRADITIONAL CLOTHING

The nearest to a Portuguese national costume is that which is still worn in the Minho. The women wear a loose white blouse with a finely worked, lace-trimmed neckline and cuffs, a full skirt with several petticoats, and a scarf around the neck or head. In chillier weather, a black shawl is added.

Many Portuguese women wear the traditional black of mourning. By tradition, black should be worn for two years in memory of a dead father, and one year for any other relative. A widow wears black for the rest of her life.

For men, the traditional look is a white, collarless shirt, perhaps with a black jacket or decorated waistcoat, black trousers, and a wide-brimmed, flat-topped black hat. Alentejo cattlemen still wear their traditional red and green stockingcaps, and the women often sport a black trilby hat to go with floral skirts.

In such tourist traps as Nazaré, the fishers wear bright tartan shirts, checkered trousers, and tasselled woolen stockingcaps, making more money posing for photographs than actually fishing. The women flaunt elaborately tied headscarves and crocheted petticoats—traditionally, there should be seven of these, and the souvenir dolls on sale usually have the requisite number! In the old days, women were expected to cover their heads and arms when entering a church. This is no longer the case, but it is still considered improper to be scantily dressed.

Folkdancer in the outfit that comes closest to a national costume for women.

LIFESTYLE

SINCE 70% OF PORTUGUESE FAMILIES live and work in some way connected with the countryside or the sea, the pattern of the seasons is part of their lifestyle. It is not possible to change springtime and harvest, they reason, so why all this fuss about being up to date?

Although there are increasingly modern influences in the bustling towns, the people as a whole are slow to leave their old traditions. This is particularly so in the northern part of the country which, unlike the south, resisted centuries of conquest by outsiders and is more insulated in its ways. It can be said that the southerners are slightly more open in their outlook. Similarly, people living in the coastal areas have had more contact with foreigners and tend to be less conservative than those living inland.

Opposite: **Fishing is both work and lifestyle for coast dwellers.**

Below: **Little girl in Madeira costume.**

LARGE FAMILIES

The mother is the accepted head of the family. In the outside world of politics and power, the voice of the woman is considered only reluctantly, but in the family the mother has the final say.

Especially in the country, large families are common. Traditionally, young people live at home until they marry; then their grandparents can help babysit. The desire to remain together as an "extended family" is easy to understand, because so many families live on their own small farms. However, as the family grows, overcrowding results and the resources of the land are taxed. This is often the reason for the large incidence of emigration from the rural areas.

People bargain over the price of goods in an open-air market.

PROBLEMS OF CHANGE

The modern age is bringing change to Portugal, but mostly in the swelling towns rather than in the conservative countryside. Statistics reveal more marriages but fewer children. Divorce is increasing, particularly among city dwellers. The Catholic Church is still opposed to contraception and abortion, but such methods of family planning are available and often encouraged in the overpopulated areas of Portugal (the Minho and central plains). Conflict between the traditions of the church and the modern needs of the economy are a worry for the staunchly religious Portuguese.

Although 98% of Portuguese will affirm that they are Catholic and that they go to church for baptisms, marriages, or funerals, there is a growing feeling that the priest is standing between them and progress. Perhaps even more so, there is a suspicion by the poor that the priests tend to take the side of the rich.

Men attend mass and confession less regularly than women. It is considered the mother's task to make offerings or vows to the saints on behalf of the welfare of her family.

Although Portugal is pleased with its democracy and has officially no royal family, the love of royalty and rank remains. The descendants of King João VI are occasionally referred to as Royal Highnesses. Those families once graced with such titles as duke or count are still respected—even though such folk may be seen in jeans and boots working their farmlands. And there are some who hope wistfully for the return of the monarchy.

WOMEN'S ROLE

There are stories of women who have made it to positions of power in politics, law, and engineering, but many women still consider themselves socially subordinate to men. A Commission on the Status of Women, founded in 1977 to defend women's rights, campaigns somewhat in vain to bring greater sexual equality. As recently as 1969, a husband could refuse permission for his wife to obtain her own passport.

A common saying is *A mulher em casa, o homen na praça* ("a-MUL-er em KAH-sa, oh OH-men na PRAH-sa"). It means the woman at home; the man in the square. Men who are not working gather in the cafés, while women sit outside their houses chatting to the neighbors. That is, when they are not whitewashing the walls—a task traditionally carried out by women.

Not until after the 1974 Revolution were women allowed to vote. They were also allowed a civil divorce (not permitted by the Catholic Church), family planning facilities, and career opportunities. In 1979 Marie de Lourdes Pintasilgo was appointed the country's first female prime minister, for a short while. But no matter what the law says, men are still paid more than women, and career women are the exception.

Families of 15 are not unusual, so there is a need for someone to play the role of caretaker. Even when sons and daughters have bettered themselves and left the country, the home, with the mother as central figure, remains a place for the family to reunite.

> "The great nations should set an example by confining women to their homes."
>
> —*António de Oliveira Salazar, in a letter to a friend*

In some rural areas, women gather in a communal place to do the day's washing.

A shepherd and his flock in the countryside.

COUNTRY LIFE

The majority of the Portuguese (70%) live a rural life, so the farm routine is the pattern of life for most families. The annual cycle of ploughing, planting, tending, and harvest are the same each year, whether the people farm potatoes in the Minho or wheat on the Alentejo plains. Vineyards in the north and fruit orchards in the south have a pattern as well. The main difference is that the northern farms tend to be smaller and family-owned, and the southern ones are more prosperous, often linked in cooperatives.

In the poorest villages of the northern mountains, livestock is centrally owned. One herd of cows, sheep, and goats is tended by shepherds who have played that role for generations. Market day is usually once a week and is often the main excitement, with the expected haggling over prices.

In the extensive rural areas, the small towns may look picturesque, with a half-ruined castle on a hill or an ornate shrine. The people gather

Fishermen mending nets in Lagos.

in the parish church on Sundays, but on weekdays they meet in the pastry shops for gossip, in the *tascas* ("TASS-cas," bars where men can get a drink), or around the school, post office, or football field. The town may lack a bookshop, but may well point proudly to the status symbol of a public swimming pool.

THE WORK OF FISHERS

In many Portuguese coastal villages there is no real harbor, so the boats must be hauled over the beach on wooden rollers. Typically, men set out in the boats, and women tend to the fish drying in the sun and supplement the family income by selling grilled sardines. The nets are dropped clear of the surf, a mile or so offshore. Then the boats return to the beach.

First the boats, then the nets, are hauled in—either by teams of oxen or by tractor. Next the catch is sorted, auctioned, and taken away. Nets are checked and mended, ropes coiled, and the oxen fed. Even in the more modern towns, where there are concrete slipways and diesel winches, there is still plenty of work for everyone.

Shops and offices line a street in the city.

AN URBAN WORKING DAY

For those in the cities, office hours are from 9 a.m. to 5 p.m., with a two-hour lunch break (from 1 p.m. to 3 p.m.). Those who have to travel to work mostly use public transport. Taxis are fairly cheap by European standards. Trains and buses are inexpensive and quite efficient, although slow. On the roads, the people drive on the right. Officially, there is a speed limit of 35 m.p.h. (60 k.p.h.) in builtup areas, 55 m.p.h. (90 k.p.h.) on open roads, and 75 m.p.h. (120 k.p.h.) on highways. Motorcyclists must wear helmets. Wearing seat belts is obligatory, and children under 12 must travel in the back seat.

Shops are usually open from 9 a.m. to 1 p.m., and again from 3 to 7 in the cool of the evening. On Saturdays everything shuts at 1 p.m.. Saturday afternoon is the time for sports (mostly soccer), and Sunday is a day of rest. Western ways are arriving, however. Some shopping centers stay open all week.

SPECIAL OCCASIONS

Baptism and marriage are great family occasions. Marriages are not arranged. The young choose freely, though usually among their own class. (Portuguese abroad nearly always marry other Portuguese.)

The *namoro* ("NAM-o-ro"), or engagement period, often starts at a dance. The formal pattern of such dances as the *vivo* and *chula* are established by courting and matrimonial traditions. The girl may be as young as 15, the boy probably three or four years older. Most couples have a long engagement period of at least three years, sometimes as much as seven or eight. The engagement is a formal relationship, during which the couple saves carefully toward the cost of setting up their own home. Usually no dowry is given, only a wedding trouseau.

The Portuguese adore a traditional "white wedding" if they can afford one, and a wedding dress trimmed with exquisite Madeira lace would be the envy of all.

At the marriage ceremony, the partners administer the sacrament to each other, no doubt with an extra prayer to São Gonçalo, the patron saint of weddings. The priest is present as a witness on behalf of the church.

Funerals are solemn, of course, but after all due respect has been paid to the departed, it is time for a reunion family tea, with jugs of wine to follow.

"It is round Bragança that the bride is still carried off from her father's house with a pretense of force, and the greatest festivals are the funerals."

—*Sacheverell Sitwell, writing of Trás-os-Montes in 1953*

The dream of most Portuguese women is to marry in a white wedding gown with all the trimmings.

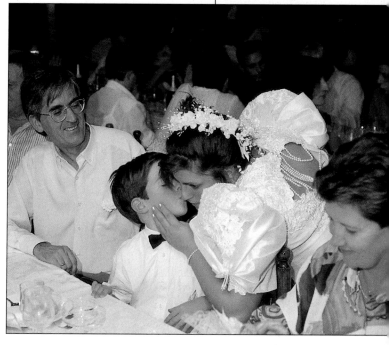

Portuguese schoolgirls. Unlike many of their mothers or grandmothers, today's women have the opportunity to continue their education right up to university level.

EDUCATION

Education has been compulsory since 1911. Preschool starts at age three and is optional. All children have nine years of schooling from age six to 15. After that, the three-year secondary education course (aimed at specific job skills) is voluntary.

One legacy from the elitist days of Salazar is a disturbingly high level of adult illiteracy, about 20%. Most of these are elderly women who have never been to school. Traditionally, the place of women was to look after the home, and education was for men. Although this attitude is long gone, its effects remain.

The present school system is not producing all the desired results. The original four years of compulsory schooling has been increased to six, then nine, but fewer than half the children complete their full nine years, for many teenagers feel the need to go to work. Only recently has the minimum working age been raised from 14 to 16. Part of the problem with education is a widespread population that requires many small schools. The other problem seems to be a lack of inspiration (and salary) among Portugal's 140,000 teachers. Yet in the country's 1990 budget, education claimed the largest share.

At the university level, the desire for education is growing. From a total of five universities in 1970, the number has grown to 19 (five private and 14 public). But admission is difficult. In 1990, close to 100,000 candidates applied for the 40,000 available university places. There are also colleges offering specialized training in such fields as cinema, music, and theater.

HEALTHCARE

In Portugal, health facilities are not as well developed as in other European countries. Since the 1974 Revolution, the number of doctors and clinics has increased. In 1979, a National Health Service that distributes free medical care was started.

Most residential areas have hospitals and clinics with a 24-hour emergency service. Many villages often rely on the local doctor. There is no lack of skill among Portugal's doctors. Professor Egas Moniz won a Nobel Prize for his work in neurosurgery. However, there are just not enough medical facilities and hospitals available for the population. Some doctors and nurses take jobs privately to supplement their low state salaries.

There are long waiting lists for treatment; scheduling an operation could take years. Those who can afford it go to private specialists and clinics; those who cannot just take the advice of their local pharmacist. In most rural areas, people rely on a combination of traditional herbal cures and modern practices.

Statistics show a birthrate of 11.5%, a death rate of 9.3%, and a high infant mortality rate: 11 of every 1,000 children die in their first year as compared to the average of nine per 1,000 for the rest of western Europe. Seventeen per 1,000 die before the age of five. On the average, men in Portugal live to 71 years and women to 78. Road accidents are a significantly high cause of death—an average of nearly 100,000 traffic accidents a year kill around 3,000 people.

A Portuguese woman's average lifespan goes well into the 70s.

HOMES

Opposite: **Living quarters in the older parts of town tend to be small and cramped, with blocks of apartments built close together.**

Below: **Apartment block in the Costa Verde town of Valenca with both shops and dwellings.**

Concrete apartment blocks are creeping into Portugal, but the bulk of the domestic architecture still retains its local character. In northern Portugal, most houses are made of granite. Animals, equipment, and the wine cellar are on the ground floor, and an outside staircase leads to the living quarters on the upper floor. In the central region, the staircase is inside the house and the walls is likely to be whitewashed and the roof made of red tiles. On the Alentejo plains, most houses are single story and gleaming white.

In the Algarve, they are just as white, often with two features of Arab origin: a lace-like chimney and a roof terrace flapping with laundry. Inside there may be countless cats.

There is a general shortage of low-cost housing, and many Portuguese still dream of owning a home with running water and a bathroom. In the back streets of Lisbon and Oporto the poverty is appalling. Thousands live in illegally built wooden shacks without proper plumbing or drains. In fact, only 58% of the population have a bath or shower in their home. Countrywide, there is a constant shortage of good housing. Although recent government incentives have helped many young couples to buy their own house, it has been calculated that there is a shortage of around 800,000 homes.

RELIGION

THE PEOPLE OF PORTUGAL hold a deep respect for the Roman Catholic Church and all its duties and festivals. Religion is the basis of family gatherings and holidays, and feast days and events are a welcome opportunity to dress in traditional finery.

FREEDOM OF WORSHIP

Portugal today enjoys official freedom of worship. The vast majority of the people are Roman Catholics. Most other beliefs—like those of the Jews, Protestants, and Muslims—are tolerated. The word "tolerated" is important, for there was a long period of time during which there was no religious tolerance.

The tortures of the Spanish Inquisition are infamous, but few people are aware of the horrors of the Portuguese Inquisition. Directed originally at the converted Jews known as New Christians, the Inquisition increased in power until it virtually ruled the country. Strict Catholicism became the state religion and remained so until 1911.

In keeping with the Catholic practice worldwide, the Portuguese consider the Virgin Mary, the mother of Christ, as a friend and protector. *Nossa Senhora* ("noss-a sen-YOR-a") is Our Lady. She is the one who will surely, if prayed to devoutly, watch over a birth, a journey, an impending death, or any family event. She is also *Nossa Senhora dos Navegantes* ("noss-a sen-YOR-a dos na-vi-GAN-tes"), guarding the sailors. She and the saints provide a way of sending petitions to God, who is generally considered too distant and powerful to be approached directly.

Opposite: **Nuns outside a cathedral in Fátima.**

Above: **Boat painted with an image of a saint to protect the sailors.**

Pilgrimages and religious festivals draw the faithful from all over the country.

Nearly all Portuguese call themselves devout Roman Catholics, although superstitious customs still linger. About a third of the people regularly attend services. For most of the citizens, the church is an important part of daily life, and in rural areas the clergy is active in local governmental, educational, and social activities. The Catholic faith also forms the basis of many Portuguese festivals, in which processions, singing, dancing, bullfights, and fireworks mark the celebrations.

Despite the people's religious ways, superstitious customs linger in many country districts. Yet the church remains the central meeting place of the parish, and Sunday services and religious festivals are looked upon as a chance for family and friends to gather and catch up on the latest news.

At Easter, the cross is taken from the church to be kissed in each house in the parish, a symbol of the new life to be shared by all.

POPE JOHN PAUL II

The words of John Paul II to the Jews, Muslims, and Protestants of Portugal: "Whatever our religion may be, the witness of faith in God unites us. We are called to proclaim religious values in a world which denies God. Our witness, our example, can help those who seek him.... To bear witness to one's faith is to contribute to the good of our neighbor, to the common good of humanity. Abraham, our common ancestor, asks us all—Jews, Christians, Muslims—to follow the path of mercy and love."

SAINT VINCENT

Cape Saint Vincent, at the far southwest corner of Portugal, is named after a Roman priest who was martyred in A.D. 304. The place was considered so holy that even the conquering Muslims allowed Christian monks to remain there. When the martyr's bones were brought there, ravens followed the ship. Again, when the remains were moved to Lisbon in 1173 (by order of King Afonso Henriques), ravens flew in escort, so Saint Vincent was proclaimed the patron saint of Lisbon. Ravens adorn the city crest. For many years, the caretakers of Lisbon Cathedral kept tame ravens, reputed to be descendants of the original birds. The last one died in 1978. Sailors say that Saint Vincent and his birds bless them as they pass.

Statue of Saint Anthony, one of the many saints venerated by Portuguese Catholics.

FOR ALL THE SAINTS

A general belief is that devout prayer to particular saints is the answer to certain problems. It would be correct, for example, to pray to Saint Lawrence if one suffered from toothache, or to Saint Bráz to cure a sore throat. Saint Christopher is specifically concerned with travelers, as is Our Lady of the Conception with infertility. Nazaré has a chapel that commemorates the miracle when Our Lady saved a 12th-century knight, Fuas Roupinho, from falling over a cliff when he was pursuing a buck on horseback. Visitors are shown "the very hoofmark" at the edge of the drop. In certain places, prayers to a certain saint seem to be answered more readily, and so national shrines develop. Pilgrimages to such shrines are a great feature of Portuguese faith.

When a prayer is answered, the saint must be thanked, or one may incur some heavenly displeasure. Such thanks often take the form of a wax offering in the shape of the organ cured, or gifts of money, jewelry, flowers, or even discarded crutches or glasses where

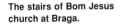

The stairs of Bom Jesus church at Braga.

these are appropriate. At Fátima, which is probably the most favored shrine in the country, so many votive offerings are presented that a special furnace is needed to burn them.

Of the many sacred pilgrimages, that to *Bom Jesus* ("bon SHAY-sus," The Good Jesus) is perhaps the most spectacular. In the woods overlooking Braga (in the Minho), this pilgrimage church of the north is reached by a great zigzag granite staircase that pilgrims climb on their knees. (For the less sincere, there is a funicular ride to the top.)

Another place of pilgrimage in the north is Penha, a sacred mountain beside Guimarães. Here among weird rock formations is an enormous statue of Pope Pius X. On a great boulder nearby is a carved memorial to Sacadura Cabral and Gago Coutinho, the two Portuguese aviators who pioneered transatlantic flying.

Tourists, rather than pilgrims, cross the plains of the Alentejo to visit the church of Saint Francis. For there in the town of Evora lies the grim *Capela dos Ossos* ("KAP-el dos OSS-os"), the Chapel of Bones. Matched bones and skulls from some 5,000 skeletons line the walls. Carved above the doorway is a reminder: "We bones that are here await yours." It is not the only such chapel in Portugal.

FÁTIMA

Near Leiria, towards the center of Portugal, stands one of the largest shrines in western Europe. There, on May 13, 1917, three shepherd children saw a vision of the Virgin Mary. A lady "brighter than the sun," dressed in a white gown and veil, spoke to them out of an oak tree and told them to return on the 13th day of each month until October.

Although the local authorities disapproved of this story, the Virgin Mary is said to have returned each month with messages of peace and advice to pray regularly. On October 13, 70,000 pilgrims waited with the three children. Many affirmed afterward that miraculous beams of sunlight shone across the sky, curing illnesses and bringing sight to the blind, but only the children saw their vision for the last time.

Fátima is now the center of religious devotion in Portugal. Vast crowds gather on the 13th of each month, and hundreds of thousands gather in May and October. Supplicants cross the huge esplanade on their knees to present their prayers at the Chapel of the Apparitions.

The town of Fátima draws pilgrims from all over the world.

75

JUDAISM

Jews first settled in Portugal in the time of the Moors. They became rich and useful to the country as bankers and financiers. Some 60,000 more arrived when Spain expelled its Jews in 1492. However, with the arrival of the Inquisition, first in Spain and then in Portugal, thousands were tortured and others burned to death for public entertainment. During one night in 1506, nearly 4,000 Jews in Lisbon were put to the sword.

Traces of the Jewish quarter, Judiaria, can still be found in many towns. The most famous is in Castelo de Vide, where Portugal's oldest synagogue, founded in the 13th century, is tucked away in a narrow, cobbled street. There is a 15th-century synagogue in Tomar. It was declared a national monument in 1921 and is now a museum containing evidence of Tomar's ancient Jewish community. The high-ceilinged hall is often used for concerts and cultural activities.

The largest Jewish community in Portugal is only about 500 and they live in Belmonte, close to the national park of the Serra da Estrêla near the northern border. In Castelo Branco, a statue stands in honor of the 16th-century Amato Lusitano, a respected Jewish doctor of medicine. There is a strong Jewish strain in this part of Portugal.

THE TIME OF THE MOORS

The Moors were skilled soldiers from North Africa who had adopted the Islamic faith of Arabia and were called Muslims. By the middle of the eighth century, they controlled all but the mountainous areas of the northern Iberian peninsula. Although some Iberians adopted Islam, much of the population remained Roman Catholic. Jews who had arrived from other Muslim-held lands were also free to practice their religion. The Moors allowed urban Jewish people—many of whom were traders, artists, and scholars—to follow their professions.

RELIGIOUS CUSTOMS AND SUPERSTITIONS

Portuguese Catholics are staunch Christians and profoundly superstitious at the same time. Each region has its favorite beliefs: that werewolves can be heard howling in the mountains, or that the father's trousers should be draped over the crib to protect a new baby from witches.

Roadside shrine in the Algarve.

On All Saints Day lamps are lit. Tombs are cleaned and decorated with flowers and visited by relatives. The people are linking with the past, praying together for the dead. In the northwest, some people say they can see a ghostly vision of a "procession of the dead," in which those who have died most recently go past carrying a coffin containing the ghost of the person who will be the next to die. The "seers" dare not reveal any names because it is believed that they will join the procession if they do so.

A religious *festa* ("FES-ta," celebration) could well mix such religious components as a procession of priests, choirboys, and acolytes carrying candles and images of saints, with such strange accompaniments as blankets and bedspreads hung from windows and balconies, and exploding rockets to frighten off devils.

Shrines with an image of Christ, the Virgin Mary, or a local saint are to be found along any country road. They are there to protect travelers or perhaps to celebrate an answered prayer. Carved along the bottom may be little flames around wretched figures that represent the souls of sinners suspended in purgatory.

MIDNIGHT BAPTISM

Of all the ancient customs in Portugal, that of the midnight baptism (practiced in the Minho region) must seem the most unusual. It concerns pregnant women—particularly those who previously suffered a miscarriage or had a stillborn child. The place must be the middle of a bridge dividing two towns or areas, thus in neither one place nor another. The time must be midnight, thus neither in one day nor another. The father and his friends guard both ends of the bridge to keep away stray animals, which might be witches or the devil in disguise.

When the church bells strike midnight, the chosen godparents must be the first people to cross the bridge. Their vital task is to pour water over the expectant mother's belly and baptize the child "in the name of the Father, the Son, and the Holy Spirit." The final "Amen" must not be spoken, for the child, now strengthened, will have its baptism completed in church after it is born.

FOLK BELIEFS

South of Guarda (the highest city in Portugal), in the Serra da Estrêla mountains, is a ring of towering crags of such daunting shapes that the town in their center has been called Sortelha, meaning "magic ring." Local superstition still fears it is the home of witches and werewolves. In the Vale de Nogueives (in the Trás-os-Montes), huge carved stones are believed to have been altars used for pre-Christian human sacrifice.

On a kinder note, folk in mountain villages often burn huge yule logs in front of their doorways or by the church porch on Christmas eve to ensure that there will be a warm place for the Christ child to be born and also to ensure that the poorest people will not be cold on that night.

On the coast north of Oporto is the small harbor of Ofir. This is the site of one of Portugal's more extravagant religious legends based on the biblical figure of King Solomon. It seems that King Solomon used to come ashore here to collect gold from the inland mines. The gold was the source of much of his fabulous wealth and was used generously to adorn his temples. In gratitude, he sent a shipload of his finest horses to Ofir, but the vessel was wrecked before it could reach land. As the horses sank beneath the waves, they were turned into stone. This may explain why Ofir is a popular spot for underwater diving!

Lonely mountain peaks seem the perfect spot around which to spin a tale of mystery or intrigue.

ANUAR

LANGUAGE

THE PORTUGUESE LANGUAGE is basically derived from Latin. The Roman invaders made sure their language was the dominant one, although changes were caused by contact with the Celtic and Iberian people. To this was added the Arab influence, which enriched the poetical sound of the language. Toward the end of the 13th century, King Dinis set up the first university, and this helped establish Portuguese as the national language. Lisbon was traditionally believed to have been founded by the Greek hero Ulysses, hence its name Lissabona. Later names of Olisipo, Felicitas Julia, and Aschbouna provide further evidence of the mixture of tongues behind Portuguese.

GROWTH OF A LANGUAGE

Language is thought in action, according to the great Portuguese poet Fernando Pessoa. Portuguese goes beyond being the language of a corner of Europe; three centuries ago it was the trading tongue of most of the ports of South America, India, and southwest Asia.

There was a time when Portuguese and Spanish were virtually the same language. Then, in the 12th century Portugal broke away from Spanish control, and its language evolved on its own with distinctively different sounds and different grammatical characterizations.

Portuguese appeared as a separate language from the 13th century. As with all languages, it remained alive and changing. As lands were discovered or colonized by Portuguese explorers, new expressions were added to the language. Even in this century, terms from French and

Opposite: **A poster announcing a bullfight.**

Above: **Road signs in Portuguese.**

81

The Portuguese share a common written language, but each geographical region has its own dialect or accent.

English (mainly technical or concerning sports) have been added.

Portuguese is correctly termed a Romance language, meaning that it has (like French, Italian, and Spanish) developed from Latin. For scholars and linguists, the Portuguese spoken at Coimbra is accepted as the language at its best. Smooth and musical, it has an elaborate sentence structure. It is for many the ideal language of lyric poetry, melancholy and sweet. Some say that Portuguese language and literature reached their richest development in *The Luciads* (dealing with the voyage of Vasco da Gama) and other works of Luis Vaz de Camões—in the same way others claim English was at its height in the works of William Shakespeare.

There is a wide range of local accents. The northern Portuguese, long cut off in their mountain villages, speak a dialect that the rest of the country finds hard to understand. Indeed, the tiny village of Rio do Onor on the northern border with Spain has developed its own dialect, music, and folk dances. But then, by way of contrast, those who live in Lisbon can hardly understand the people of Algarve (where many speak English anyway).

From the beginning of this century, there were calls to simplify and standardize the spelling of Portuguese. In 1953 the governments of Portugal and Brazil approved a new system: *f* was substituted for *ph, t* for *th,* and *i* for *y.*

WHO SPEAKS WHAT?

The language of Portugal is also the language of Brazil, Angola, Mozambique, Cape Verde, São Tomé and Principe, East Timor, and Guinea-Bassau. Portuguese is the base tongue from which many Creole languages have grown. There are large communities of Portuguese speakers in the United States, France, and South Africa. It is the seventh most widely spoken language in the world.

There are four recognized Portuguese dialects: those of northern, central, and southern Portugal, and the Brasiliero of Brazil that has had added input from the Tupi Indians and African slaves. About two million people in northwest Spain speak a Portuguese dialect called Galician.

On their own mainland, almost all Portuguese understand Spanish in addition to their own language. Children are taught both French and English. Although shopkeepers and tourist guides show off their linguistic abilities, most Portuguese expect visitors to learn a little Portuguese. How else can the courtesies of greeting be exchanged?

Young people learn Portuguese, French, and English in school.

83

The town of Cascais in Portugal.

HOW TO SAY THE WORDS

The pronunciation of Portuguese words is very different from their written form. The syllable to be stressed is not always the first syllable—Setúbal, for example, is pronounced "sh-TOO-bl." Portuguese has nasalized vowels, somewhat similar to French. Syllables ending with *m* and *n* often sound as if they ended with *ng*. So *sim* (yes) is pronounced "SEE-ng," but without sounding the *g*. The same sort of sound is created by the tilde accent (that wavy line over a vowel), as in *ã*, *ão*, and *ães*.

The cedilla accent, *ç*, comes under a *c* and gives it a soft sound. So *graça* (grace) is pronounced "GRASS-ah." If the *c* does not have a cedilla, it sounds hard. So *pico* (top) is pronounced "PEE-koh." *S* sounds like *sh* before a consonant or at the end of a word. Thus Cascais is pronounced "KAHS-kaish." This gives Portuguese a rather slushy sound. The letter *j* sounds like the *s* in the word "pleasure." The letter *g* often sounds the same as *j*, unless followed by *a* or *o,* in which case it is hard.

GREETINGS

Traditional courtesy is a strong feature of Portuguese communication. Everyone expects to be treated with dignity. Greetings and manners tend to be elaborate. "Your Excellency" is a common form of address. Lawyers, doctors, and university graduates are addressed respectfully as *Senhor Doutor* ("SEN-yor DOO-tor") for men, and *Senhora Doutor* ("sen-YOR-a DOO-tor") for women. Even such titles as *Excelentissimo Senhor* ("EX-se-len-TISS-i-mo SEN-yor") or *Excelentissima Senhora* ("EX-se-len-TISS-i-ma sen-YOR-a) are used widely.

Despite such courtesies being widespread, there is an underlying obstinacy among some people to ignore them—or to allow their more modern-minded children to do so. There is a Portuguese expression *por se suas tamanquinhas* ("por se SOO-as ta-man-KEEN-as"), which means "to put on your clogs," in other words, to move slowly or be obstinate. This comes from the leather country boots called *tamancas* ("ta-MAN-kas"), which have a thick wooden sole.

"It is the sort of language that sounds like verse even when the speaker is merely discussing the validity of a motor insurance policy."

—*Patrick Swift* in Minho and North Portugal

Hello	*Ola* ("OH-lah")
Good morning	*Bom dia* ("bawng DEE-er")
Good evening	*Boa noite* ("boa-er NAWNG-ter")
Thank you	*Obrigado* ("oh-bri-GAR-doh") for men; women say *Obrigada*
Please	*Por favor* ("poor fa-VO-ar")
Yes	*Sim* ("SEE-ng")
No	*Não* ("NAH-ng")
Goodbye	*Adeus* ("er-DAY-oos")
Come back soon	*Até breve* ("er-TAY BRAY-ver")

ARTS

WHERE DOES ONE START? With Portuguese folklore that has found expression in music, literature, painting, and singing, from the cheerful, rhythmical songs of the Minho region to the grand and woeful *fado* ("FAH-do," folksongs) of Lisbon and the Alentejo.

There is folklore too in handicrafts: the delicate embroidery of Madeira, the famous china of Vista Alegre, the crystals of the Marinha Grande, ornate gold or silver filigree jewelry, or Arraiolos carpets.

Craft workers in the humblest villages use patterns and skills whose origins are lost in time: the decorated linen of Guimarães; the richly carved ox-yokes that change design and shape in each region of the Minho, local pottery painted electric blue, pottery made from black clay, intricate paper flowers, and in many brightly colored forms, the Portuguese emblem of the cockerel.

Opposite: **Worker in a Costa Verde ceramics factory.**

Above: **The cockerel emblem is synonymous with Portugal.**

COCK OF BARCELOS

A popular legend relates how a pilgrim on his way to Compostela in Spain was accused and found guilty of theft as he left the town of Barcelos. He was sentenced to the gallows, all the while proclaiming his innocence and praying to Saint James.

His last cry for justice was a claim that a roast fowl on the judge's dinner table would rise and crow in proof. The miraculous bird duly returned to life, crowing loudly and allowing the man to live. Bright red and black pottery roosters are available as souvenirs and are popular with tourists all over the country.

Luis de Camões, author
of the epic poem, *The
Luciads.*

LITERATURE

The songs made up by traveling minstrels in the Middle Ages are part of the birth of Portuguese literature, for they combine well-informed commentary on the events of the day with an appreciation of style and word-play. Poetry, in its different styles, has always been appreciated in Portugal. In the 15th century, court chroniclers began to record Portuguese history, but all books were still handwritten. It was the invention of printing, coinciding with the Renaissance, that allowed literature to expand and flourish.

The many plays of Gil Vicente established Portuguese theater: religious dramas rooted in medieval style, mysterious tragicomedies with historical themes, and broad comic satires poking fun at everyday life in 16th-century Portugal. Poets experimented with the Italian sonnet form. Luis Vaz de Camões was among the leading poets, and is remembered most for his patriotic *Luciads.* The excitement of exploration and sea discovery is reflected in much Portuguese writing.

In the 18th century, the Enlightenment spread through Europe, with fresh thinking on education and science. In Portugal, a style called neoclassicism became popular, returning to the pure power of language in reaction to the exaggerated verbiage of the 17th-century baroque. Among such social comment came the satirical poetry of Barbosa du Bocage, who lived riotously and wrote irreverently. Romanticism followed, with the lively plays and novels of Almeida Garrett and the historical novels and poems of Alexandre Herculano. The romantic ideal in Portugal was to create a new country.

A fresh realism heralded "the generation of the 70s." Scholarly argument from the university town of Coimbra resulted in the publication of *Bom Senso e do Bom Gosto* (*Good Sense and Good Taste*), a now famous discussion in print of late 19th-century literary attitudes. (It is interesting to note that Hans Christian Andersen visited Portugal in 1866 and considered the country "the stuff of fairy tales.")

The word *saudade* ("sow-DAH-de"), a sad longing for the past, is essential to understanding much Portuguese writing. Fernando Pessoa, one of Portugal's greatest poets, indulged often in this nationalistic nostalgia. He used various pen names according to his mood. In that way he could be romantic, wry, heroic, or comic—all styles used in his writing.

Portugal is proud of its authors. Famous names include José Eça de Queiroz, a novelist with wit, invention, and a polished style; Fernando Namora, an internationally famous novelist; Alves Redol, whose book *Gaibeus* about the harsh life of migrant laborers has gone into its 17th reprint; the communist novelist José Saramago; Almada Negreiros, poet and painter; Viterino Nemésio, whose novel *Mau Tempo no Canal (Bad Weather in the Channel)* written in 1944 is still considered outstanding; and the nonconformist poet Manuel Alegre.

Unfortunately, reading is not a popular pastime in Portugal. The price of books and the struggle to earn a living limit the funds available for buying books. Such showpiece libraries as the baroque fantasy in Coimbra University seem to have books on display for their impressive bindings rather than for actual reading.

"I feel myself multiple. I am like a room with innumerable mirrors that turn into false reflections."

—Fernando Pessoa, on his poetic writing

THE LUCIADS

This epic poem is a song of praise to the greatness that was Portugal. Like Homer's *Odyssey,* it is the story of a man and also of national pride and glory. *Os Lusiadas (The Luciads)* tells of Vasco da Gama's sea voyage to India in 1497 and pays homage to Portuguese bravery and the spirit of adventure. It is named after Lusus, the companion of the god Bacchus, who by legend was the first settler in Portugal.

Its author was Luis Vaz de Camões (also spelt Camõens), an impoverished nobleman who was unwise enough to dedicate a love sonnet to one of the queen's ladies-in-waiting whom King João III also favored. Banished from Lisbon, he became a soldier and saw action in North Africa, where he lost an eye. After service (and imprisonment for street fighting) in Goa, Macau, and Mozambique, he scraped together enough money to return to Portugal in 1570. He was there when the vainglorious King Sebastião attempted his disastrous invasion of Morocco. The Luciads express the general sadness that the glory of Portugal was vanishing forever. Although his lyric poetry earned him only a small pension in his lifetime, Camões is venerated as the national poet of Portugal.

Opposite: **The National Theater of Dona Marie II in Lisbon.**

THEATER AND CINEMA

Live theater throughout the world has suffered financially from the competition of cinema and television. So too, the once proud theatrical tradition of Portugal has faded, dependent almost totally on subsidies offered by the Theater Fund and the generous Calouste Gulbenkian Foundation. In the 1950s, the Oporto Experimental Theater worked valiantly. Then in 1974 the abolition of censorship enabled theater groups to aim at a new popular audience.

The first Portuguese film was made in 1896, and determined producers have continued to fight for popular support and official subsidies. Box office records are held by Antonio Pedro Vasconcelo's *O Lugar do Morto (Place of Death),* which attracted 130,000 viewers in 1984. Portugal's most respected filmmaker is Manoel de Oliveira, but even his work has eluded the Oscars and film festival prizes of other European directors.

Now that the National Theater of Dona Marie II in Lisbon has been rebuilt after being gutted by fire, there has been a fresh interest in drama. The film world has not prospered so well; only a half-dozen films are made in Portugal each year.

The ornate Palace of Pena in Sintra.

ARCHITECTURE

Portugal offers Celtic fortifications, Roman temples, a few Moorish buildings, plenty of Arab influence, medieval castles, and churches in every style from stern Gothic to encrusted Baroque.

As Christianity recaptured the peninsula, so churches were built in celebration using the Romanesque style then popular in Europe. Built mostly out of carved granite, the churches have simple shapes: semicircular arches, smooth round pillars, and often a cross-shaped plan to the building. The pointed Gothic arch became popular in the 13th and 14th centuries, giving the strength for added height and increased gracefulness.

A combination of Romanesque, Manueline, and Renaissance architecture can be seen in the Convent of Christ overlooking Tomar on the plains northeast of Lisbon. Built first as a castle, this was the headquarters of the Knights Templar, originally a religious order founded to fight the Muslims

MANUELINE

Such terms as Romanesque and Gothic are used to describe architectural styles all over Europe, but only in Portugal will you find the Manueline style of architecture. Named after King Manuel I, in whose reign the style came to its peak, this is almost oceanic art: exuberant yet delicate decoration that stems from the worldwide exploration by the Portuguese in the 15th and 16th centuries. Its main feature is stone carving, linking maritime themes with motifs from heraldry and Moorish design. Pillars twist like barley sugar in the fashion of ship's cables, and buildings are decorated with a profusion of ropes, knots, anchors, globes, pearls, shells, and the military cross of the Order of Christ.

The Manueline influence can be seen in the Monastery of Jeronimos (shown here), a religious monument containing the tombs of Camões and Vasco da Gama. It can also be seen in the Abbey of Batalha (Battle Abbey), built to commemorate victory over the Spaniards at Aljubarrota in 1385. Prince Henry the Navigator is buried there among fantastic carved traceries, like lace made of stone.

and protect the Holy Sepulcher in Jerusalem. However, their military strength became a threat in Europe, and they were expelled from France and Spain. Many took refuge in Portugal, where in 1320 King Dinis gave them a new title, the Order of Christ. After the king's death, they lost their military status and become monks.

Portuguese architecture next adopted the exuberance of the baroque closely associated with King João V. This found expression in gilded woodwork, ranges of stairways (as at Bom Jesus in Braga), twisting pillars, and a colorful use of *azulejos* ("a-zoo-LAY-shoss," or ceramic tiles).

Toward the end of the 18th century, a neoclassical style with Greek and Roman colonnades became popular, but Portuguese love of the romantic still found expression in such strange buildings as the Disney-like Palace of Pena, in Sintra, and the wildly ornate Palace Hotel of Bussaco. A few equally strange Art Nouveau buildings emerged in the early 20th century, mostly in Lisbon and Coimbra.

The Place Marquis de Pombal in Lisbon has in its center a sculpture of the Marquis de Pombal, who supervised the re-construction of Lisbon.

PAINTING AND SCULPTURE

Much of the early art and sculpture of Portugal was religious in subject, because the church was the great patron of the arts. Panels (called triptychs) intended to stand behind an altar showed saints and biblical scenes, and sometimes the faces of donors (who provided funds for the building of the church or the creation of the artwork) were painted in among a watching crowd. Carving inside and outside churches and on royal tombs was of impressive quality, such as the gilded woodwork in the church of St. Francis in Oporto.

As politics took center stage in history, so sculptors created monuments and artists turned to celebratory portraits. No visitor to Lisbon can fail to be impressed by the Monument to the Discoveries by Leopoldo de Almeida, showing Prince Henry the Navigator at the front of a line-up of famous Portuguese explorers.

Often following the same styles as architecture, Portuguese art expressed itself in Neoclassical eminence with Vieira Portuense, blending with Romanticism in the dramatic, almost mystical work of Domingos Antonio Sequeira. Columbano Pinheiro was a masterly portrait painter in the early 20th century, and his brother Rafael set up a porcelain factory that virtually became a school for ceramicists. Among today's leading artists are Vieira da Silva, Julio Pomar, and Paula Rego; among sculptors, José de Guimarães and Jorge Mealha.

DECORATIVE ARTS

Any country that has been invaded by Muslim conquerors seems to inherit an appreciation of and skill in geometric decoration. The greatest national art form of Portugal is probably the glazed tiles (*azulejos*) that adorn walls everywhere. Other skills include delicate gold jewelry, furniture with gilt engraving and often Oriental details, blue and white porcelain from Aveiro in imitation of earlier imported Chinese chinaware, rare Arraiolos carpets influenced by Persian design, and striking stained glass.

Azulejos tiles at Our Lady of Piety church.

Every local market displays crafts, whether hand-painted pottery, tapestry cushions, wallhangings, copper coffeepots, or shaped baskets.

AZULEJOS

There is a national passion for covering the walls of buildings—churches, palaces, restaurants, and railway stations—with blue and white ceramic tiles. Even ordinary houses are covered with striking tiled designs. The use of decorative tiles was introduced to Portugal by the Moors. The name *azulejos* comes from the Arabic *al zuleiq* ("ahl zoo-LAYK"), meaning a small polished stone. Though some are multicolored and some more classical, with white background and feathery gilded borders, the favorite colors remain white and blue (colors introduced by Dutch artisans). Clay in square molds is fired at high temperatures, then painted with oxides: copper for green, cobalt for blue, antimonium for yellow, manganese for brown, and tin for white. There is a National Tile Museum in Lisbon showing the history and changing skills of making *azulejos*.

MUSEUMS

Portugal (particularly Lisbon) is rich with museums. The pride of them all is the Calouste Gulbenkian Museum built to house and display the thousands of priceless objects and works of art collected by the Armenian millionaire and given to his adopted country. The collection ranges from Egyptian ceramics and gold coins from ancient Greece through medieval manuscripts and tapestries, to paintings by Rembrandt, Watteau, Turner, Manet, and Renoir. There is also Chinese porcelain and French Art Nouveau. The building also houses a concert hall, library, and snack bar.

Lisbon's other museums cover interests in ancient, modern, decorative, folk, and religious art; archeology; military and naval matters; and *azulejos.*

CALOUSTE SARKIS GULBENKIAN

This generous supporter of the arts was an Armenian born in Turkey. He assumed Iranian citizenship during World War II and made his fortune by negotiating oil concessions between the United States and Saudi Arabia. He adopted Portugal as his country during his last 13 years, living on one whole floor of a central hotel in Lisbon until his death in 1955.

With his priceless collection of Eastern and French art as its nucleus, the Gulbenkian Foundation has established a historically important art collection. It also runs a cultural center that brings first-class music, ballet, and art to the city.

MUSIC AND DANCE

The chants of church worship, the songs of troubadors, and singers at the royal court were part of the growth of music and traditional dance forms in Portugal. King João V, rich with gold from Brazil, hired a group of Italian singers under Domenico Scarlatti, and so opera arrived in Lisbon. In the 18th century, the performances of João Domingos Bomtempo introduced the Portuguese to the music of Haydn, Mozart, and Beethoven. Not long after, Portuguese-born John Philip Sousa made his name in the United States by composing *Stars and Stripes Forever* and inventing the musical instrument known as the sousaphone.

Among Portugal's more modern composers are Luis de Freitas Branco and Fernando Lopes Graça. There is a National Broadcasting Symphony Orchestra in Lisbon. The Portuguese enjoy concerts too, and these are often staged in cathedrals, palaces, and ruined castles. The concert might feature a popular pianist such as Artur Pizarro.

LEISURE

THE PORTUGUESE TAKE LEISURE time seriously. The midday siesta time is used whenever possible. Meals take a long time. Weekends are sacred. The few shops that do open on a Saturday morning close promptly at 1 p.m. The rest of the day is there to enjoy sports, stroll the parks and gardens, or join the *fado* singing in a wine shop.

The Portuguese consume, per person, over 100 liters of wine a year—which puts them in the top five in Europe. In Algarve and the south of Portugal, the custom lingers on (a practice from the Moors) that women should not enter *tabernas*. It used to be improper in Oporto for women to ask for port, so they would order "cold tea" and the port would be brought to them in a teapot!

SPORTS

The Portuguese take part in various sports either as participants or spectators. To be daring in sports became a national characteristic centuries ago. For example, in 1709 Bartolomeu de Gusmão, a Jesuit priest, invented a flying machine that he named *Passarola* ("pas-sa-ROH-la," or Big Bird). It actually rose off the ground, and the Portuguese public named him *Voador* ("voh-AH-dorh," or the Flyer). However, his invention did not receive royal patronage, so Portugal missed the chance to become the first airborne nation. But it can claim the first air crossing of the South Atlantic in 1922. Sacadura Cabral and Gago Coutinho flew from Santa Cruz to Brazil in a tiny airplane—five years before Charles Lindberg's more famous solo crossing in 1927.

Opposite: **Woman crocheting.**

Below: **Leisurely conversation over port wine at a** *taberna.*

Athlete Carlos Lopes is one of Portugal's most outstanding sports personalities.

Soccer dominates the sports scene for men, and thousands of fans pack the stadiums. Athletics and gymnastics are popular with women.

The marathon champion Rosa Mota is a national heroine. She won the bronze medal at the Los Angeles Olympics in 1984, the first Portuguese woman ever to earn an Olympic medal. She did not disappoint her fans and went on to win the gold medal at the Korean Olympics in 1988. But her early training days were accompanied by shouts of shame, for it was not considered correct for a woman to be seen in public wearing shorts. Not only that, but she also relates how people used to call after her: "A woman's place is in the home. Go and cook, go and wash the dishes!"

Since then the people's attitudes have changed, and in 1994 the Portuguese women's team won the World Cross-Country Championships at Budapest.

Among male athletes, Portugal salutes Carlos Lopes, who won the Olympic marathon in Los Angeles, and sprinter Fernando Mamede who established a world record in the 10,000 meters in Stockholm in 1984. But facilities in general are lacking for athletic training.

There are 17 golf courses, 11 of which are of world championship standard. Vale do Lobo and Quinta do Lago in the Algarve are perhaps the most famous, and golf there is played the whole year round. National golf championships are held twice a year. Tennis is becoming more popular, and many hotels have built clay courts for their guests in addition to the local tennis club. Water sports and ice hockey are both popular, too.

Forty-one percent of Portugal's coastline has beaches (about 500 miles, or 800 km, of sand). Colored flags warn of strong undertows on the Atlantic coast, although there is no such warning for polluted water near industrial sites or off the over-used Algarve. In the mountainous areas, people have opportunities to fish or hike, or go horseriding in the cool, clean air.

For those who want more adventure, the spirit of daring lives on. Fairly recently, a daredevil in Oporto dived off the Dom Luis bridge to break the European record for a bungee jump. With the help of a 200-foot (60 m) crane on top of the bridge, he jumped a total of 295 feet (90 m).

Motor racing attracts the crowds at the Estoril Autodrome, near Lisbon, where there is an annual Formula One Grand Prix. Since 1984, many top racing teams have used the Estoril course for testing and training, and such drivers as Nelson Piquet, Alan Prost, and Ayrton Senna have been regular visitors. Vila Real is the motorcyling capital of Portugal, with international events in June and July.

In the Portuguese colony of Macau off the Chinese mainland the streets downtown are cordoned off in November for the annual Formula Three Grand Prix. Formula Three cars have smaller engines, lower weights, and narrower wheels than Formula One cars.

Estoril's Grand Prix race is an annual event that draws large crowds.

SOCCER

Futebol ("FOO-ti-bal") became popular in Portugal during the reign of King Carlos (who ascended the throne in 1889) and has become as vital to the Portuguese as baseball is to the Americans. Devoted fans fly in from far away to watch top teams Benfica or Sporting (both of Lisbon) or FC Porto. Sporting won the Portuguese title seven times in eight years (1947–54). Then Benfica established itself as one of Europe's finest teams in the 1960s, winning the European Cup in 1961 and 1962 and reaching the final three more times in the next six years. In 1987 Porto won the European Cup, the World Club Cup, and the European Super Cup. Most Portuguese support one of these three teams. Of the lesser local teams, FC Guimarães offers fair competition to the big three.

Portugal's most famous soccer player, Eusebio, was born in Mozambique and was six times the leading scorer in the Portuguese League. Playing for Portugal against North Korea with his team 0-3 down, Eusebio took over: he scored four goals himself and paved the way for the fifth.

In the 1928 Olympics, the Portuguese soccer team came in fifth. Portugal also captured third place in the 1966 World Cup in England, came close in Mexico in 1986, and was beaten by a single goal in the last minute in the 1984 European Cup in France.

Portuguese soccer player Eusebio (right) has become a legend in his time.

BULLFIGHTS

The bullfights of Portugal are different than the gory affairs of Spain. The main action is conducted on horseback, a contest of elegance, daring, and skill, as a *cavaleiro* ("ka-val-EYR-o") controls his highly trained horse so that he can plant a dart in the bull's neck. There are different sizes of darts and different ways they can be placed.

After the *cavaleiro* has planted the darts, a team of eight *forcados* ("for-KAH-dos") takes over on foot, wrestling the bull with their bare hands. Ever since the death of the Count of Arcos, who was gored to death in public in 1799, it has been forbidden for a bull to be killed in any fight. Instead, a gesture is made with a wooden sword to indicate the animal's defeat. However, most bulls have been wounded too badly to survive, so they are butchered out of sight afterward.

There are over 30 bullrings in Portugal. The main one is Campo Pequeno in Lisbon, built of red brick in a pseudo-Moorish style.

In Portugal, bullfight scenes are pictured everywhere, from postcards to *azulejos* decorating the walls of the market.

FADO

Here, in what was simple folksong, is the soul of Portugal. Supposedly evolved from ballads sung by homesick sailors, *fado* (meaning "fate") is an emotional, though not necessarily unhappy, music. It is a time after dinner to sit and contemplate the glory that once was Portugal. The singing is full of that essential Portuguese quality, *saudade,* or bittersweet nostalgia. The *fadista* ("fa-DIS-ta") sings alone, usually accompanied by guitars—either the 12-stringed Portuguese *guitarra* ("gi-TARR-a") or the more common western viola. The most famous *fado* singer of all was Amália

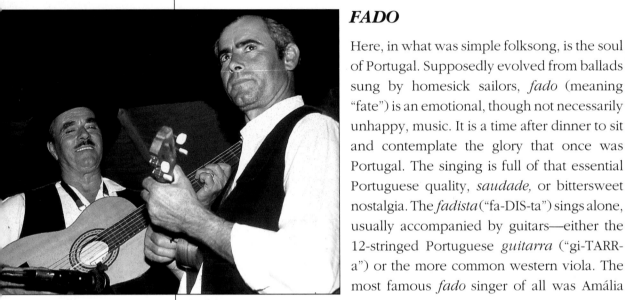

Dinner and folk music go hand-in-hand in some restaurants.

Rodrigues.

Many *fado* houses now cater to tourists. They levy an entrance fee, serve dinner, and charge high bar prices. Singing does not start until around 10 p.m.

POPULAR MEDIA

Everyone watches television, either for sports or for the soap operas, called *telenovelas* ("te-li-NOH-ve-las"). They watch in cafés, bars, restaurants, and in homes. Television and radio licenses are paid as a percentage of the electricity bill. There are many imported shows (including *Dallas*), which are usually given Portuguese subtitles, keeping the original soundtrack. The main channel, RTP (*Radiotelevisão Portuguesa*), was controlled by the state until 1990. Then, amid great public argument, private radio stations were sanctioned and two private television channels

NA PAZ DOS ANJOS: UM ELENCO DOS DIABOS.

A sua nova telenovela do fim-de-semana - Canal 1

Telenovelas feature local and imported fare.

were introduced that included air time for the Catholic church.

Portugal has about 400 cinemas, but attendance is on the decline thanks to television. Imported films are shown in their original language with Portuguese subtitles. There are 25 newspapers (including seven on the Azores and five on Madeira) as well as over 1,000 other periodicals.

FOR THE YOUNG

There are youth hostels throughout Portugal: bicycling, hiking, and mountain climbing are increasingly popular with the young. Over 100 campsites and caravan parks are to be found in woodland areas or near the sea, although these are used more by tourists than by locals.

Two Portuguese organizations are affiliated with the World Scout Movement. The Association of Scouts of Portugal (founded in 1913) has some 48,000 members in the standard age groups of Cubs, Scouts, Seniors, and Rovers. There is also a separate Scout Corps that is a coeducational Catholic association.

FESTIVALS

SOMEWHERE IN PORTUGAL most weekends of the year there will be a festival, often held in honor of a locally venerated saint. The festivals range from religious processions and pilgrimages to celebrations with folk singing and dancing. There may also be floral displays, fireworks, or bullfights. Traditional outfits are often worn. Processions may parade oxen through the streets (as in Moncão at Corpus Christi), or feature lines of women carrying baskets of rose petals (as in Vila Franca do Lima for the Festival of Our Lady of the Roses).

Opposite and below: **Girl and women in colorful outfits taking part in festival celebrations, which usually include a street parade.**

NATIONAL HOLIDAYS

Since Portugal is an overwhelmingly Catholic country, most of its national holidays are the official feast days of the church, some of which vary from year to year. June 10 is the main national holiday. Officially it is the Day of Camões and the Community. The "Community" was added after the bloodless 1974 Revolution, and the day still celebrates (as did the poet Camões) the national pride of Portugal. It is also called Portugal Day. The national anthem is *A Portuguesa*, written by Lopes de Mendança in 1890.

On April 25 the country celebrates the anniversary of the 1974 Revolution. Red carnations are the symbol of this happy event because the soldiers put carnations in the barrels of their rifles. Some people still have the flowers carried on that day, carefully dried and preserved. December 1 marks the restoration of Portugal's independence from Spain.

If a festival falls on a Tuesday or Thursday, many businesses also close on the Monday before or Friday after, making a long weekend, known in Portugal as a *ponte* ("PON-ti," or bridge).

PILGRIMAGES

The people go on a *romaria* ("roh-MAH-ri-a"), or pilgrimage, to a shrine or sacred place to gain favor from the saint whose festival or feast day they are celebrating. At one time pilgrims walked all the way and camped out in the woods. Nowadays they go by bus. It is a colorful, cheerful occasion as they approach the shrine. Drums, pipes, and accordions may play; banners and floral decorations provide extra color; and there may be a special platform for dancing.

Pilgrims gather to observe a religious event amid pomp, pageantry, and fanfare.

Crowds flock to Viana do Castelo (in Minho) to celebrate in the name of *Nossa Senhora de Agonia* ("NOSS-a sen-YOR-a da a-go-NEE-a"), Our Lady of Agony. For one week, women parade in widow's black or flame-colored floral costumes, and the word *amor* ("a-MOR," or love) is emblazoned everywhere. After a religious procession on Friday, the people follow with a parade of decorated floats through the town with drum-pounding bands, folkdancing, and plenty of wine. Fireworks sparkle each night. On Monday the fishing boats are blessed, and the streets around are decorated with pictures in colored sawdust.

The Douro valley around Oporto sees a folk-style pilgrimage to São Gonçalo at Amarante in June, and at Whitsuntide a three-day pilgrimage to Matosinhos. Thousands come from Galicia in Spain to Soajo to celebrate the festival of *Senhora da Peneda* ("sen-YOR-a da PEN-i-da"), or Our Lady of Penitence, showing that the *romaria* is older than the frontier. The greatest pilgrimage of all, however, is to celebrate the visit of Our Lady to Fátima in May or October.

*"I could hardly
sleep for the
jingling of bells,
beating of drums,
and flourishings of
trumpets which
struck up at
daybreak in honor
of that pompous
festival, the Corpo
de Deos."*

—*William
Beckford in his*
Portuguese Journal,
1787

Opposite: **Color, cos-
tumes, and fun at a street
carnival in Funchal, Ma-
deira.**

SPECIAL DAYS IN A YEAR

Many festivals and fairs have their origins in pagan celebrations of springtime or harvest, old year or new. On the island of Madeira, *Fim do Ano* ("fin do ANN-o," or the end of the old year) begins in the capital city of Funchal on December 8. Children sow seeds of wheat, corn, or lentils in moss or wet cotton fibers to sprout in time for Christmas. Each house is whitewashed and decorated. Honey and almond cakes are cooked, and spicy liqueurs are brewed. There is a replica of the Nativity scene in every church and home. The Portuguese share with the Chinese a love of gunpowder, so the last night of the old year is ablaze with fireworks, spectacular in Madeira, and popular on the mainland as well. Then it is *Ano novo!* ("ANN-o NOH-vo," or Happy New Year) to all.

There is a Mimosa Festival in Viana do Castelo every Sunday in February, when the whole town is golden with blooming mimosa. Women in traditional dress sell handicrafts, and there is folkdancing in the streets. Carnival time in the cities comes on the Monday and Tuesday before Lent begins on Ash Wednesday. Huge, colorfully decorated floats trundle through the streets, and hotels hold dinner dances to liven the night. Then comes Easter, with the bullfighting season opening on Easter Sunday.

June, the midsummer month, is the time of the popular festivals of Saint Anthony, Saint John, and Saint Peter. Song and dance resound all night. At Sintra, near Lisbon, Saint Peter's Day has the biggest fair of the year, with local produce and handicrafts.

At the end of September, the whole country rejoices in the grape harvest. Then, on November 1, comes the Day of the Dead, particularly meaningful for the Portuguese, since on November 1, 1755 a great earthquake destroyed much of Lisbon. Tombs are scrubbed clean. Jars of flowers are brought in and candles lit.

FOOD

PORTUGUESE COOKING is as adventurous as its explorers were. Portuguese traders returned home with the first shipments of coriander, ginger, saffron, and paprika. Pepper, cinnamon, and curry powder came from India and are now staples in Portuguese cooking.

The Portuguese were the first to introduce rice and tea to Europe. From Africa came coffee and peanuts, while pineapples, chilis, tomatoes, and potatoes were brought in from the new lands discovered by Portuguese navigators.

Portuguese cooks sometimes use many spices at once (in contrast with their Spanish neighbors, who use little spice) and add cream and butter to make the food richer. At times the cooking is exotic in its boldness, using borrowings from far-off places to experiment with foreign tastes. Spices from the Orient, a peppery flavor from Brazil, and the art of using sugar from Turkey all form part of the Portuguese cook's menu. One unusual cooking utensil is the copper *cataplana* ("ka-ta-PLAN-a"), a hinged cooking pan shaped like a clam.

The best restaurants are in Lisbon; some of them are family-run *tascas* where the mother presides over the stove and the father waits on table. It is acceptable to order half-portions, even for adults, as normal helpings tend to be enormous. Many menus list the price of half-portions, usually at two-thirds of the full rate.

Portugal's annual National Gastronomy Festival is held each autumn in the small farming town of Santerém in the Ribatejo, 43 miles (69 km) up the Tejo River from Lisbon.

Opposite: **Market in the Algarve selling fresh fish.**

Below: **Mussels cooked in a *cataplana*.**

EATING HABITS

Fish, fresh or dried, and many forms of shellfish are popular. But prices are rising, and poorer families make do with homegrown vegetables made spicy by the addition of a few slices of garlic-flavored sausage. The popularity of the cheap, backstreet *tascas* remains high. These simple eating places often provide some of the best food in Portugal.

Portuguese cooking would be impossible without olive oil. They pour it over potatoes and dried cod and cook with it most of the time. Although there are modern mechanical processes to create and refine the oil, traditional stone wheels are still used in rural parts of the country.

Most Portuguese blend their own coffee. Even a modest shop will offer a choice of 15 to 20 different beans and roasts. A strong, dark cup of coffee, called a *bica* ("BI-kah"), is often drunk together with a glass of port. Tea is drunk too, rather weak, in the style that Catherine of Bragança introduced to her husband King Charles II of England—so starting the English's habit of taking afternoon tea. It is called *chá* ("cha"), copied from the Chinese word for tea—possibly the origin of the English "cup o' char," meaning "a cup of tea."

DAILY MEALS

Meals shared by the family are an important part of Portuguese daily life. Most Portuguese take a light breakfast of rolls and coffee. The midday meal will include soup, fish or meat, plenty of vegetables, and a rich dessert. The habit of taking a snack with a glass of wine in one of the many *tascas* is popular. This may be enough for the evening, or there may be a fuller dinner around 8 or 9 p.m.

SOUPS

Portuguese cuisine is famous for its filling stews and soups. Friendly arguments persist on what is Portugal's "national dish," but a clear contender is *caldo verde* ("KAL-do VAIR-di"), a green soup made from thin shreds of tender, deep green cabbage.

The cook boils potatoes, onion, and garlic in stock and olive oil, then rolls cabbage leaves into a fat cigar shape and shaves off slices with a sharp knife. These are dropped in only a minute or two

Caldo verde is a rich vegetable stew cooked with thin slices of smoked sausage.

before serving, with thin slices of smoked sausage. Cornbread is sometimes crumbled into the soup. The result, served in a large bowl, is very thick and tasty, and often eaten with a fork.

This *caldo verde* is the specialty of Minho in the north. So too is the shellfish *açorda* ("ass-OR-da"), a dish of softened bread with oil, garlic, and whatever mussels, clams, or prawns were netted in the catch for that day. The bread is soaked in the liquid used to cook the shellfish, and this turns the soup into a filling dish. Chopped coriander is often added for extra flavor.

Pigs are raised on the plains of the Alentejo, and there they eat *sopa alentejana* ("SOPP-a al-ENT-ish-AH-na"), a soup of chopped bacon, smoked ham, coriander, and onions. This is served with a slice of bread that is topped with an egg poached in the hot soup.

COD

There are, they say, 365 ways to cook cod. So popular is this fish that it is known as *o fiel amigo* ("oh FEE-al a-MEE-go"), the faithful friend. *Bacalhau* ("bok-kel-YOW") is dried cod, which has to be soaked in water overnight before it can be cooked. It used to be the poor person's staple; today it is more expensive. Whereas sailors used to dry the cod on the deck as they sailed home, nowadays everything caught is frozen. Portuguese shops even import dried cod from Norway to supply determined customers. But there is still fresh cod to be eaten, baked on top of newly sliced potatoes in plenty of garlic oil, served sprinkled with fresh parsley. Sometimes the fish is flaked and mixed with potato salad, bits of onions, tiny bits of hardboiled egg, and lots of black olives and olive oil. And there is the tasty *bolinhos de bacalhau* ("bol-EEN-yohs de bok-kel-YOW"), patties made from dried cod—never to be referred to as "fish cakes!"

SEAFOOD

Soups are memorable in Portugal, but fish is supreme. Bought at early-morning fish markets, the freshest fish and shellfish are stewed in a dark brown sauce (with cumin, chopped parsley, tomatoes, garlic, and onions) to make *caldeirada* ("kal-dey-RAH-da"), the heavy-tasting fish stew served in every coastal town. Every seaside street has a vendor grilling sardines to sell as a tasty snack.

From the sea come sole, bass, red mullet, hake, swordfish, and squid. From the freshwater rivers come lampreys, salmon, eels, and trout. The Portuguese never tire of their many-flavored fish dishes. And, to the surprise of foreigners, they drink red wine with their sardines and dried salted cod. They mix fish with meat too, cooking pork with clams and stuffing trout with smoked ham.

MEAT

Portugal is not a land for those who love steak. The lack of grazing land for cattle and the poor conditions in which sheep and goats are raised mean that most meat dishes are cooked long and slowly, often marinated in a wine sauce to make the tough meat more tender. But pigs abound in the cork-oak forests of Alentejo, and much of the pork gets turned into garlicky sausages or delicate smoked ham.

Regional dishes include Oporto's *dobrada* ("dob-RAH-da"), tripe stewed with beans, chicken, pigs' trotters, and other ingredients; *carne de porco à alentejana* ("KAR-ni da POR-ko a al-ENT-ish-AH-na"), a classic meat dish of the Alentejo plains with chunks of pork seasoned in wine, coriander, and onions, and served with clams; *leitão* ("lay-TAN"), suckling pig served in the vineyards of Bairrada; *iscas* ("ISS-kas"), the pan-fried liver popular in Lisbon; and *churrascos* ("choo-RASS-kos"), or chicken barbecues, brushed with *piri-piri* ("PI-ri PI-ri," chili pepper), a more modern habit that started in the Algarve.

Suckling pig is the specialty of the town of Mealhada in Beira Litoral, 12 miles (19 km) north of Coimbra. There are at least a dozen restaurants serving it.

Other meat dishes include partridges, pigeons, and quail, where these game birds can be found. Most dishes in Portugal are served with either rice or fried potatoes; salads usually include lettuce, watercress, tomato, and pimento.

Poor grazing conditions for cattle and sheep result in lower quality meat.

CHEESE

Most cheeses in Portugal are made from sheep's milk, although hard yellow goat cheese is made as well. In the villages, it is still squeezed in cheesecloth so that the whey (juice) drips out and then is left to dry and grow a thick rind. The result is often rock-hard and bun-shaped. It may be creamy smooth in taste, or dry and peppery, with the taste of the herbs that the sheep eat on the mountains. Soft cottage cheeses (such as those from Tomar and Azeitão) are moist and eaten sprinkled with pepper and salt. Restaurants often serve a portion of cheese as a starter or to freshen the palate between courses. The best cheese, it is said, comes from the Serra da Estrêla.

Sausages, cheese, and port to whet the appetite.

SWEET DESSERTS

Common desserts are *crème caramel* ("krem ka-RA-mel") with toffee-flavored sauce, and rice pudding served sweet and sprinkled with cinnamon. Cake and coffee shops do a brisk trade—and the Belem cake shop in Lisbon, built in 1837, still sells cakes baked in a special way and served hot with sugar and cinnamon.

Convents are often famous for making sweets such as the *ovos moles* ("OH-vos MOH-les") made of egg yolk and sugar and molded into the shapes of shells and fish. Sometimes the egg yolk is soaked in syrup or mixed with ground almonds, and it is always formed into miniature shapes of fruits, birds, animals, or geometric designs. Some sweets have curious names: *papos de anjo* ("PAP-os da AN-yo," angels' breasts), *orelhas de abade* ("O-REL-yas da a-BAH-di," abbot's ears), and *barrigas de freiras* ("ba-REE-gas de FREY-as," nuns' bellies).

For fruit, the Portuguese can choose from pears, oranges, plums, figs, and apricots. Grapes, of course, come in many varieties. From the Azores come pineapples; from Madeira, custard apples and passionfruit.

CODFISH BALLS

1 cup dried salted cod
2 cups cooked mashed potato
½ tablespoon butter
Pinch of black pepper

Wash the fish in cold water and cut into small pieces. Cook in boiling water for about 20 minutes until soft. Drain and mix thoroughly with the mashed potato, butter, and pepper. Shape into small balls and put each into a pan of oil. Fry six at a time for about one minute. Drain on absorbent paper. Serve either hot with cooked tomatoes or cold as a snack or appetizer.

The picturesque Vila Mateus, from which the Mateus Rosé wine takes its name.

WINE

The famous wines of Portugal can be considered under three main headings: table wines, Madeira, and port. The pink, slightly sparkling Mateus Rosé has gained fame abroad, and its potbellied bottle now travels worldwide. This delicate wine is named after Vila Mateus in the Trás-os-Montes region—a curlicued Baroque palace placed by a geometrical lake amid vine-terraced hills.

A smooth, red wine is produced in the Algarve, and several areas around Lisbon make wines (including a sweet dessert wine called Moscatel). The bulk of Portuguese wine comes from the Douro valley near Oporto and the hills of the Minho. The *vinho verde* produced here is unique to Portugal. The name means "green wine," but that is not its color; it refers to the young quality of the grapes used. The wine has a slightly bubbly quality and the flavor varies from refreshingly fruity to very dry and tart. The white goes well with richly flavored fish dishes and the

PORT

The story told is that port wine was "invented" by two young wine shippers from Liverpool. Back in the late 17th century wines were brought to Oporto in wineskins on the back of mules. To preserve the wine during this rough treatment, one of the young men had the idea of adding some brandy and, so it is said, port wine was born. It is still sometimes called "the Englishman's wine."

Certainly trade in this wine resulted in the first firm links between Portugal and Britain. The British did not wish to lose their supplies of Oporto's rich, red wine (though port wine can also be white). When British shippers, greedy for profit, started adding all sorts of colorings and additives, the Marquis de Pombal made laws to regulate production of the wine. Exact areas were demarcated and control placed totally under the Alto Douro Wine Company. Later the amount of brandy added was also limited.

Some port wines are aged in wooden casks, others are bottled and labeled with the year of vintage. The quality varies from year to year, and certain "vintage years" are much prized, fetching high prices. Most of the port lodges (some of which store wine dating back to 1811) are across the river from Oporto city. At the Port Wine Institute in Lisbon, several hundred varieties of port wait to be sampled.

red with thick soups or peppered pork. Clean and clear, it is allowed to ferment in the bottle, usually with a pinch of sugar added at the bottling.

A most unusual wine is produced only in one remote northern village. In 1809 the villagers of Boticas buried their wine to hide it from the invading French armies. Dug up a year or two later, it tasted even better, so they continued with the custom. It has gained the name of *vinho dos mortos* ("VEEN-yo dos MOR-tos"), the wine of the dead.

Another famous wine is Madeira, named after the volcanic island where it is grown and bottled. It is a fortified wine (given longer life by the addition of distiled alcohol) and has a unique, nutty flavor. There are four main styles, sercial ("SIR-sial") and verdelho ("vair-DEL-o"), which are dry on the tongue, and bual ("BOO-al") and malmsey ("MARM-si"), which are sweet and rich.

There is also bottled and draught beer. Sagres is the most popular draught, known as "imperial." Of course, the Portuguese also drink water. Tap water in municipal areas is clean, but the people prefer the bottled variety of mineral spring water.

The way to drink port: "Ruby with sardines, vintage with candlelight."

—*Local saying in Oporto*

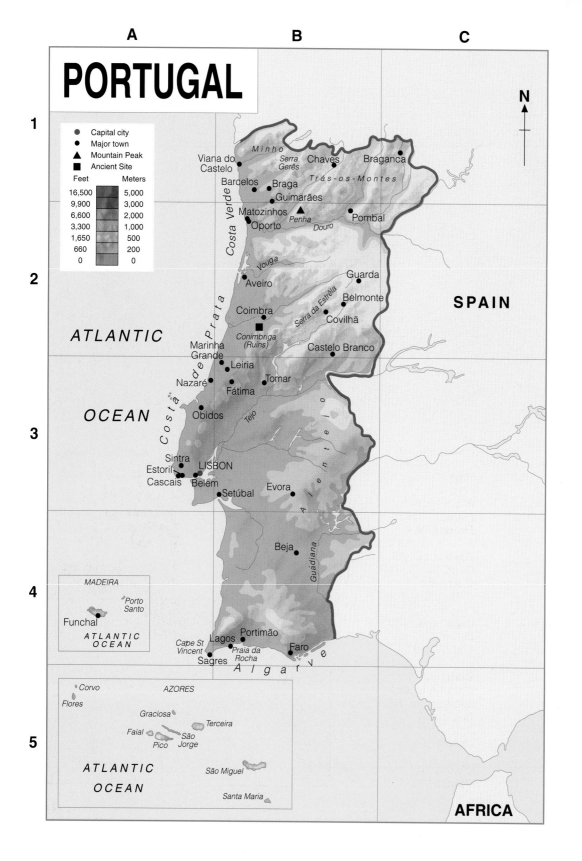

PORTUGAL

N

Legend:
- ● Capital city
- ● Major town
- ▲ Mountain Peak
- ■ Ancient Site

Feet	Meters
16,500	5,000
9,900	3,000
6,600	2,000
3,300	1,000
1,650	500
660	200
0	0

ATLANTIC

OCEAN

SPAIN

Minho

Viana do Castelo

Serra Gerês

Chaves

Bragança

Trás-os-Montes

Barcelos

Braga

Guimarães

Costa Verde

Matozinhos

▲ *Penha*

Oporto

Douro

Pombal

Vouga

Aveiro

Guarda

Coimbra

Serra da Estrêla

Belmonte

Covilhã

Conimbriga (Ruins) ■

Castelo Branco

Costa de Prata

Marinha Grande

Leiria

Nazaré

Fátima

Tomar

Obidos

Tejo

Sintra

Estoril

LISBON

Cascais

Belém

Setúbal

Evora

Alentejo

Beja

Guadiana

MADEIRA

Porto Santo

Funchal

ATLANTIC OCEAN

Cape St Vincent

Lagos

Portimão

Praia da Rocha

Faro

Sagres

Algarve

Corvo

AZORES

Flores

Graciosa

Terceira

Faial

São Jorge

Pico

ATLANTIC

OCEAN

São Miguel

Santa Maria

AFRICA

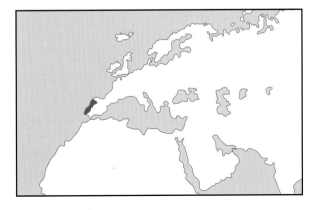

QUICK NOTES

LAND AREA
35,516 square miles (91,986 sq km), including Azores and Madeira

POPULATION
10,525,000 (including Azores and Madeira)

CAPITAL
Lisbon

LAND REGIONS
Minho, Trás-os-Montes, Douro Litoral, Beira Alta, Beira Litoral, Beira Baixa, Estremadura, Ribatejo, Alto Alentejo, Baixo Alentejo, and Algarve (traditional but not official)

MAJOR RIVERS
Tejo, Douro

MAJOR LAKES
Guadiana

HIGHEST POINT
Serra da Estrêla, 6,532 ft (1,991 m)

NATIONAL FLAG
Two vertical stripes of green and red, the green occupying two-fifths of the total area; superimposed on the stripes is the state coat of arms: a white shield containing five small blue shields, each bearing five white disks, in the form of an upright cross, with a red border containing seven yellow castles, all placed against the background of a yellow sphere.

NATIONAL SYMBOL
Cockerel

OFFICIAL LANGUAGE
Portuguese

MAIN RELIGION
Roman Catholicism

CURRENCY
100 centavos per escudo
(US$1=158 escudos)

MAIN EXPORTS
Textiles, footwear, timber, pulp, automotive parts, and cork

IMPORTANT ANNIVERSARIES
April 25   Liberation Day
June 10   Camões Day
October 5   Republic Day
December 1   Independence Day

POLITICAL LEADERS
Mario Soares (president)
Anibal Cavaco Silva (prime minister)

LEADERS IN THE ARTS
Luis de Camões (poet)
Fernando Pessoa (poet)
Gil Vicente (playwright)
Vieira da Silva (artist)
Artur Pizarro (pianist)
Amália Rodrigues (*fado* singer)

GLOSSARY

Algarve
Coastal region in the south of Portugal.

azulejos ("ah-zoo-LAY-shoss")
Glazed ceramic tiles that adorn buildings throughout Portugal.

bacalhau ("borh-kerhl-YAO")
Dried salted cod.

bica ("BI-kah")
A strong, dark coffee.

caldo verde ("KAL-do VAIR-di")
A green soup made from cabbage.

cataplana ("ka-ta-PLAN-a")
A hinged cooking pan shaped like a clam.

caravel
Speedy 60-foot ship with a triangular rig, designed by Prince Henry's navigation experts.

escudo ("ess-KOO-do")
Portuguese unit of money.

fadista ("fa-DIS-ta")
Folksinger.

fado ("FAH-doh")
Nostalgic folksongs.

festa ("FES-ta")
A celebration.

graça ("GRASS-ah")
Grace.

Marranos ("ma-RAN-os")
Jews who were forced to convert to Christianity but practiced Judaism in secret.

namoro ("NAM-o-ro")
Formal engagement period preceding marriage.

pousadas ("poo-SAH-das")
Historic buildings that have been turned into guesthouses.

retornados ("re-tor-NAH-dose")
Portuguese who have emigrated but are forced by circumstances to return to their homeland.

romario ("roh-MAH-ri-o")
A pilgrimage.

saudade ("sow-DAH-de")
A feeling of homesickness or nostalgia.

vinho verde ("VEEN-yo VAIR-di")
A young wine.

BIBLIOGRAPHY

Klan, Marion. *The Portuguese: The Land and its People*. London: Viking, 1991.

Lerner Publications. *Portugal—In Pictures*. Minneapolis: Lerner Publications, 1991.

Moore, Richard. *Portugal*. Austin, Texas: Steck-Vaughn, 1992.

Solsten, Eric. *Portugal, a Country Study*. Washington: U.S. Government Printing Office, 1994.

INDEX

INDEX

INDEX

PICTURE CREDITS